ALSO BY CHELSEA HODSON

*Pity the Animal*

*Tonight I'm Someone Else*

# Tonight I'm Someone Else

ESSAYS

## Chelsea Hodson

HENRY HOLT AND COMPANY    NEW YORK

Holt Paperbacks
Henry Holt and Company
*Publishers since 1866*
175 Fifth Avenue
New York, New York 10010
www.henryholt.com

A Holt Paperback® and ® are registered trademarks of
Macmillan Publishing Group, LLC.

Distributed in Canada by Raincoast Book Distribution Limited

Library of Congress Cataloging-in-Publication Data

Names: Hodson, Chelsea, author.
Title: Tonight I'm someone else : essays / Chelsea Hodson.
Description: First edition. | New York : Henry Holt and Company, 2018.
Identifiers: LCCN 2017053407 | ISBN 9781250170194
Classification: LCC PS3608.O4747 A6 2018 | DDC 814/.6—dc23
LC record available at https://lccn.loc.gov/2017053407

Our books may be purchased in bulk for promotional, educational, or
business use. Please contact your local bookseller or the Macmillan
Corporate and Premium Sales Department at (800) 221-7945, extension
5442, or by e-mail at MacmillanSpecialMarkets@macmillan.com.

First Edition 2018

Designed by Meryl Sussman Levavi

Printed in the United States of America

1   3   5   7   9   10   8   6   4   2

As the surgeon's scalpel reveals my organs, love introduces other versions of myself, whose obscene novelty disgusts me.

—ÉDOUARD LEVÉ, *Autoportrait*

# Contents

*Tonight I'm Someone Else*

Red Letters from a Red Planet

## 1. Spring

In Tucson, I rode my bike until the heat turned into something else, something alive, something I could make my own—my cheeks flushed red, I sweat out any water I drank, and I didn't care—that was just how I moved from one place to the next in ninety degrees. I lived in a house so old I told people it was haunted, even though I didn't have any proof. I liked finals week, when the library was open all night and no one knew where I was. I didn't keep a journal then. I was busy, or I thought I was, but mostly I thought anything important would stay with me. Perhaps it has.

The team's second machine had already been catapulted toward Mars by the time I started working at the operations center. Their first attempt had exploded after failing to land a few years prior. It would take nine months to find out for sure, but this one, they said, would make it.

*Phoenix*—or, as I wrote in press releases later, NASA's *Phoenix* Mars Lander—was on its way to the planet's northern hemisphere, the polar region. Its robotic arm was designed to reach out and dig through the dirt until it found water ice, but no one knew for sure what lay beneath. It was 2008, and no one had ever sent anything to the top of the Red Planet. I was an undergraduate studying journalism, and the public affairs manager needed an assistant.

I would help her write image captions that went out with the press releases each day. As the lander sailed through space, the team assembled at a warehouse in Tucson and waited.

From the porch at my friend's party one night, I heard the *shhh shh* of spray-paint cans. When I looked at the wooden fence across the street, I could see men in hooded sweatshirts with their backs to us, moving their arms up and down, painting their names.

They walked toward the party, pulled their hoods down and their sleeves up, exposing their tattooed arms and filling the porch with leftover fumes. Cody was the most memorable of them—I'd admired his pronounced brow bone from across a room before. I've always liked men who look as if they're from another time. We'd been introduced once at The Grill, the twenty-four-hour diner with blue walls and a neon sign that read, Open Later Than You Think. On the porch at the party, he said, *I'm Cody*, and I said, *I know who you are*.

Downtown was vacant at night—not even the police bothered as Cody and his friends wrote all over everything as if they owned it. In the mornings after, a hired worker always appeared in some form, holding a white roller and a bucket. Sometimes Cody would get there before they did, and he could take a picture in the daylight before his name disappeared under more paint. One building for one night—that's all some men get.

Cody and his friends rode around town like royalty until everyone began actually regarding them as such. Crowds parted to make way for them on the sidewalk, and bars banned them for fighting, which just made them more infamous. Seeing one of them meant the rest were somewhere nearby. They ruled downtown, filling the spaces their fathers had left behind—men betrayed by cops, some jailed, one killed.

Cody's earlobes were long and saggy and had holes the size of quarters from the ear gauges he'd once worn. In the backyard of someone's birthday party, he told me he didn't wear the gauges anymore, and soon someone was going to sew his ears back up to look normal. *I'll miss them*, I said, sitting on his lap, taking the cap from my beer bottle and placing it inside one of the holes. I'd never been attracted to someone I was afraid of before, but I could tell Cody was tender because he couldn't look me in the eyes when I became bold and touched him. He was big and tough and tattooed, like a bad boy a casting director might dream up, but when he kissed me, it felt specific.

Cody banged on my screen door like a warning, and I always answered. It felt good to be summoned. One time he came over in the middle of the day to meet my friend who was visiting from out of town. He didn't sit down, he just paced around my living room while I tried to make conversation. After a few minutes, he pointed at his backpack on the floor, said, *I have to deliver that*. I asked, *Drugs?* and he smiled, said, *I'll never tell*, then left.

I gathered secrets like little pieces of survival, and I was so healthy. I never knew the whole story, just enough to be on their side. One of his friends slept on my couch one night while cop cars rolled through our neighborhood's streets, looking for him. Another of his friends went to Nogales and almost didn't get back in at the border. I knew fighting was bad, but I was so in love with Cody, I believed what he believed: that some people deserved to get hit. The men thought their badness made them special, and I thought my devotion to their self-imposed justice made me special, and I think we might have both been right.

At work, I milled around the operations center drinking free espresso some company donated because they thought we were astronauts. I was the only one who bothered with the espresso—I even had an argument with an engineer who told me drip coffee was more powerful. No one knew what to do except pretend to prepare—the lander soared through space, and we were on the verge of either everything or nothing. It was a part-time job for me, but some men's lives had led up to this landing, and they'd failed before.

In preparation for the landing, my boss and I helped the team rehearse what to say to the public, who might not understand the timing. *Make sure to explain that the signal could come later*, my boss said. *It doesn't always reach us right away.*

During finals week, I reached for my highlighter pen to stripe my geology textbook yellow. I was learning about my own planet—its tensions and the resulting shifts. I liked the inevitability of nature, the violence required for Earth to endure. The lecture hall was filled with a hundred students, but the professor had asked that we all e-mail her a photo of ourselves so she could memorize us. She actually did it, and I found myself frightened every time I raised my hand and realized she still knew my name.

The halls of the operations center were empty most of the time. Or if I did encounter someone and met their gaze— even if I greeted them—they'd usually look away. The lander was getting closer after its nine-month, 140-million-mile journey, but there was still nothing to do yet. I pretended to be a scientist; the scientists pretended to work—or they did work, I just didn't know what they did.

The *Phoenix* lander was seven feet tall and eighteen feet wide and weighed 772 pounds. On May 25, 2008, we all gathered in the operations center and waited for *Phoenix* to descend into the Martian atmosphere, activate its heat shield, and slow to one thousand miles per hour. The lander survived what everyone called its *seven minutes of terror*—a free fall, a blue parachute—and then it landed the way we'd hoped it would. The solar panels bloomed and sucked in light. The ovens adjusted their temperature. The machine photographed its feet and sent us the picture.

When the images appeared on-screen an hour later, the room erupted in applause. I felt like an impostor—how had I gotten there? When I noticed everyone around me was crying with joy, I tried to do the same. I'd never felt I was in the same room as history before.

The following day, I heard someone at a press conference say, *We will find water; it is there.* It was the same tone I used to announce that I loved who I loved.

## 2. Summer

Cody was tall, but his posture was terrible, as if he hadn't fully evolved. For this reason, I could spot him blocks away when I was on my bike, and then I'd get to spend whole minutes doing nothing but anticipating him. When he changed a record on the turntable in my apartment, he'd spin the record on his finger and tell me to watch. He was good at it—the record seemed to play from electricity he made. I remember he was the first man I told, *I love your body.* I don't remember what he said about mine.

I was always asleep by the time he got into bed and draped himself over me, finally done tagging—another night of not getting caught. In the morning, I always woke up before him, but I'd stay under him for as long as I could, memorizing his tattoos, as if someday I might need to describe them so he could be found and returned to me, the one who knew his entire body by heart.

Once, just after midnight, he came over with bloody knuckles and torn jeans. It wasn't unusual for him to bleed, but it was the first time he'd come to me afterward. I found a translucent purple ruler in my desk, broke it in half, and made a splint to keep his ring finger straight. He told me the story as I washed the red from his hands, his shirt, my floor. He kissed me on the kitchen counter, threw my phone across the room when it rang. I didn't yet know who I was, but I saw the opportunity to become a certain kind of woman. Harm swayed toward me. I responded with something else.

The Martian day, called a *sol*, is forty minutes longer than an Earth day. That meant we came to work a little later each day and stayed a little later, until soon we were arriving in the middle of the night. Photographs came in hours ahead of me—as a series of zeros and ones.

*Phoenix*'s cameras worked better than anyone had anticipated. One evening, the lander captured an image of the sunrise after Mars's seventy-five-minute "night." The photo looked straightforward, but the image's caption explained, *The skylight in the image is light scattered off atmospheric dust particles and ice crystals.* We thought we knew exactly what we saw.

At The Grill one night, a painter looked at me too long, and Cody asked him to rate the importance of his hands: *You use them a lot, I bet.* Another night, Cody pointed to a red bicycle's crumpled front tire, locked to a fence, and said, *That's where his head was.* If I was alone at a bar and someone approached me, one of the graffiti men would appear and ask, *Is this guy bothering you?* and I'd say no, because he'd already be gone. I felt safe in their small-town grasp, special, but really I was just on one side of my mind and the world was on another.

When I needed a ride one night, one of Cody's friends drove me home in his powder-blue Cadillac, asked, *What were you doing out so late?* As the streetlights shone through the windshield, I saw the gun on his hip, glittering. In Arizona, it was legal to carry a gun as long as it was visible, Wild West style. We passed the hotel where John Dillinger left $23,000 in a fire in the 1930s, the same hotel where this friend with the Cadillac had been blacklisted. I admired the way they maneuvered through the world, making it theirs.

At the Phoenix Science Operations Center, a group of sleep researchers from Harvard came and installed blue boxes on our desks. One group of scientists was instructed to look directly into the simulated sunlight for an hour each day. One group was asked not to look at all.

I used to sit at the bar still wearing my school backpack, sipping whiskey Cokes and pretending not to hear what any of the men said. But I did hear, and once I was asked, *Do you think it's wrong to cut off a finger?* I said no, not if someone really deserved it.

Even now, I feel compelled to protect their identities in a noir kind of way—to refuse to give them up, even under interrogation. I want to see them again. Sure, I was an accessory, a warm body, a room to sleep in, but I felt as if I was a whole building being written on. Their violence was blinding, their light immeasurable. Every time I tried to take a photo of anyone, they'd look away, or appear as an orb, as if I'd dreamt them up.

But a dream does not leave blood on the pillowcase, does not get into bed smelling like spray paint and other women, does not write his name on a wall or my thigh, does not finish high school or ask for forgiveness. They were waiting to get rich. Every time it rained, we knew another year had gone by.

There was a replica of the *Phoenix* lander at the operations center. It was built to scale, looked real. When I gave a tour to a middle-school class, one student looked at the lander and asked, *How will it get back to Earth?* and I said, *It won't.*

Many of the photos I captioned were actually composites of photos—different cameras captured different angles, and the images needed to be put back together. By the time I saw them, they appeared whole.

### 3. Fall

When photos showed strange clusters of dirt on the Martian plain, one of the scientists said, *We expected dust devils, but we are not sure how frequently. It could be they are rare, and* Phoenix *got lucky.*

Most nights, Cody expected to get caught painting his name. *One day I'll run out of luck,* he said, not stopping.

There was a rumor that the cops kept binders full of graffiti photos, organized by name, in the hopes they'd catch that name someday. A friend of Cody's friend got caught writing on a freeway sign, and, in court, the prosecution showed dozens of the same signature on other walls. He went to jail for all the photos combined. The men wondered if they had binders dedicated to them. They smiled when they talked about it.

*NASA's* Phoenix *Lander Might Peek Under a Rock*—that was one headline. The team thought there might be ice there. The robotic arm reached out.

I met a man who complimented me all the time, but instead of feeling admired, I felt nervous. I realized Cody and his friends never seemed to look directly at me. There was comfort in that. Sometimes it felt like a favor.

Alice was the name of the rock near the lander. Snow White was the name of the trench *Phoenix* began digging. The robotic arm dug a little more each day. And then, after fifty scrapes, a white square appeared—what the scientists had hoped to find. The soil-and-ice mixture was scheduled to be dropped into an oven, then cooked. They called the sample *almost perfect*.

But the arm was imprecise, the movement was wrong, and the sample missed the oven. From the press release: *We will repeat what we did successfully with small modifications to adjust for what we learned.*

I'd learned almost everything about Mars by that point—the temperature, the presence of the icy layer, the wind speed—but when I tried to describe Cody to a friend who had never met him, all I could say was, *He has this pull on me.* I mimed myself unloading an imaginary rope from my stomach, kept unloading it. My return to my previous life had always seemed inevitable, but now I felt so far away.

These were men who fell in love but not fully, wanted a mother but not really, wanted a whore but not all the time, wanted me in the room but quiet, and I liked trying to be everything at once. Cody said he wanted the word *honey* tattooed on his throat, and when I asked why, he said, *To remember everyone I ever called honey.* I said it was a bad idea, but really I just wanted to be the only one called honey, I wanted to be the word he kept in his throat.

### 4. *Winter*

The operations center tried to contact *Phoenix* on Mars, but we didn't hear back. We countered silence with another press release: Phoenix *was not designed to survive the dark, cold, icy winter.* Still, we listened.

I started to believe Cody's friend with the Cadillac would eventually be caught. I saw men get hurt, jump fences, get handcuffed, go to jail. He'd been arrested twice before for other things; another seemed inevitable. One day, he noticed a man sleeping in an unmarked police car across from his house. Another followed him to work. This is how these things end, I thought, remembering a movie. I could get left behind so easily.

I saw a scientist place a black piece of paper over the blue box of light, then pull it up slowly, say, *Total eclipse.*

I knew about the trio of girls with frizzy black hair and greasy eyelids, but I didn't know they'd come for me. Their cutoff shorts exposed green-purple bruises, their purses were big enough to carry forty-ounce bottles of Mickey's. I liked to drink, too, but not like that—they didn't care if they died or not, they didn't care who belonged to whom, they'd show up to parties and suddenly there'd be a bonfire in the backyard, suddenly they'd be lighting their cigarettes with it. One of them got cancer at one point, lost all her hair, and lived.

*Cody and I slept together,* one of the girls said to me on the phone one night. *I didn't know you were still together.* I didn't bother raising my voice with someone who seemed as if she was telling the truth, someone who seemed sorry. I asked logistical questions: Did he wear a condom? He did. Did she know about me? Sort of. I thought if I had information, I could have control. I thought if I stayed calm, I could keep it from being true. I waited for Cody to come home.

When I confronted him, he had me call his friends to confirm her unreliability. *She's just jealous,* a few of them said. Others deemed her plain crazy. Cody seemed to think the more people we called, the more innocent he'd be. I knew he was guilty, but I stopped fighting it and started listening to the sound of their lies. They became like a chorus of men who loved each other. They were singing their song.

In the morning, she texted me, *I'm afraid you believe whatever he told you*, and it was true—I loved him enough to look away. That's how much he loved me. We were even.

A caption for a photo of morning frost on Mars: *This false color image has been enhanced to show color variations.*

I put Cody in an essay once before, but I wrote it wrong: I made him the villain. I forgot women can be wrong, too—I forgot I could be. Against all logic, I perceived touch from a burned hand as a form of greatness. I hope to make a mistake like that again someday.

*Phoenix*'s signal officially died when ice appeared on its solar panels. The attempts to reach the lander were called *listening campaigns*.

From the press release: *The* Phoenix *spacecraft succeeded in its investigations and exceeded its planned lifetime. Although its work is finished, analysis will continue for some time.*

We cleaned out our desks, wiped our hard drives, went out for lunch, ate french fries covered in ranch and bacon bits. The principal investigator of the *Phoenix* mission said to the press, *Somewhere in that vast region there are going to be places that are more habitable than others.*

Some men never loved me. I didn't care. Their names sounded like answers, and I used them as such.

In one of the last photos received from *Phoenix*, its solar panels looked like an umbrella protecting the—I want to write *earth* here, but that's incorrect. The red dirt made everything red. Then the photos stopped.

Cody kept staying out all night. I kept not saying anything, kept thinking eventually he'd come back to me for good. My room was too bright for sleep, so I held my pillow over my face, exhaled into the black of it. I saw beautiful things.

# Simple Woman

Sexiness dates. Beauty, on the other hand, does
well with a touch of the archaic: it does not
need us.

—JAMES RICHARDSON, *Vectors*

The fancy gym near Bryant Park in Manhattan costs $220
a month. I bought my membership online, late at night,
without thinking too hard, looking for something to make
me happy. Money can do that if you let it—if you close your
eyes and enter its dream, the one where you are well
dressed, fit, successful, in love with exactly the right person. The gym I used to belong to cost $30 a month, but
sound judgment gets lost so easily in unhappiness: the new
price seemed justifiable because I would have paid almost
any price to become a new person.

The treadmills at the fancy gym offer a selection of videos to
watch while I run. The videos I scroll through on the touch
screen include scenes from faraway cities, forests, deserts. I
forget I'm in a basement, running in place, or at least that's
the idea. Some of the scenes go places only a drone can go:
the tops of cliffs, jumping from one balancing rock to the
next, or through a flooded canyon. I pay to use the treadmill even though I could run outside. It's not the same.
Running outside is full of cars ignoring red lights and men
calling out to me and unforgiving concrete. Running outside is real, but what I want is the less real: I want the

path unfolding on a screen in front of me, I want to run through a place I've never been.

I never used to exercise, not even when I was modeling. The only kind of preparation I did then was to stop eating the day before. There was always food available on set, but no one cared if I ate or not, they only cared about the way I fit into the clothes and the ways in which I angled my body in front of the camera. I liked it that way.

What I miss most about modeling, besides the money, is the way I was touched on set. Someone was always helping me step into clothes, or putting them over my head so my makeup didn't transfer onto the collar, or pinning the clothes tight against the back side of my body, clips invisible from the front. I miss the way a makeup artist would be brushing my face with powder while another stylist fixed my hair, arranging it so that just the right amount fell in front of my shoulders versus the back. My mother used to lightly touch my head or my arms when we watched television together, and the touch of stylists brought me back to that place of my childhood.

When I first started modeling, my only tricks and methods were from *America's Next Top Model*—smile with your eyes; put your hands on your hips and arch forward like a hunchback if you're wearing couture; model with your whole body, all the way down to your fingers and toes. But as I got older, I narrowed it down to one trick, one simple, private action: think of someone you want to touch whom you cannot touch, someone forbidden. Think of a room where there is nothing except the two of you: still, you cannot touch them. Think of the heat between two hands about to touch, the language that exists in that silence. Now, turn the camera into the face of the beloved and tell it everything without speaking. You might think this is too subtle, but, if you live in your mind, the heat of your longing can be captured on film. I have proof.

I can look at photos now and remember who I was thinking about that day. It's so obvious. My longing sometimes kept me up at night, which was the opposite of what I wanted: to dream. I bought a white-noise app on my phone, turned on the thunderstorm setting, and closed my eyes.

Money is a dream, which makes it as real or as unreal as the rest of my life.

Dream logic seems fine for a world that has been theorized to be nothing more than a simulation—a big video game where we think we play the world, but in fact someone else plays us. I buy what I can't afford; I idolize people who have nothing to do with me; I refuse to believe one thing leads to another, which is to say I don't believe in logic, not all the time—not the way this world rotates and orbits. I feel slower than it, too poor to live in it; I want to sleep until I'm someone else.

Modeling sometimes felt like a way to make up for all the status I'd missed out on as a child. Now I could be the one.

When I paged through magazines as a teenager, I assumed every model was a wealthy star.

I've never had a job that had benefits of any kind—health insurance, sick days, stock options. Jobs like that always felt like traps to me. I understood, though, when my friends got in and then couldn't get out. It was safer than my erratic life and unpredictable income. But I thought I'd never have to struggle to get out if I just never got in.

I've worked for enough millionaires to know that more money doesn't mean more happiness. But facts were never enough to cancel out my dreams. Wake me up from a nightmare and try to tell me it's not real. Try to tell me more money wouldn't fix my life.

When I was very young and my mother picked me up from a wealthy friend's house, I said in front of both mothers, *Her bedroom is bigger than our entire house!*

I never have fantastic dreams with elaborate landscapes and neon colors. My dreams usually take place in small, plain rooms and have very little action: it's about the dialogue. I sometimes wish I could unhear it, I sometimes resent my subconscious for its self-destructive tendencies. Like the trance I enter when I am engaging in masochistic behavior (picking at my skin in a magnifying mirror, looking at the Instagram profile of someone I despise): time stops; I enter a space where nothing else matters except the action I'm conducting right there, right then. Nothing could be more important than hurting myself in these small, private ways.

I like that phrase I kept hearing when the eclipse happened: *path of totality*. I didn't have eclipse glasses, I wasn't in the right city to see the sky go black, but I watched the live stream from my iPad in Bryant Park. There was something emotional about it, even within my virtual disconnect—something about the perfection of one black circle covering one white circle. How is it that we were born on just the right planet at just the right time? How is it we know exactly when and how to look up? How is it we never remember how small we are until a planetary event arrives, and how does this realization move so quickly from comfort to assault?

In my dreams, there are no planets, just bodies, no ring of light, just the promise of something, which, now that I think about it, might be the same thing.

I have listened to music I hated until I loved it. I have looked at ugly clothes so long they began appearing as desirable objects. I have lived in America so long that money started to seem like a good idea.

We assign meaning to money the same way we assign meaning to dreams. By that logic, money could be a dream. And what else would it be? I always want more of a good dream, but how quickly a nightmare descends.

I assign meaning to love as well. So could money be love? No, because it doesn't linger. As soon as the desired object is purchased, the heat of the wanting is transferred elsewhere.

In 2007, I really wanted a job at American Apparel. I was living in Tucson then, and I had been working in retail for a couple years at that point. I even became one of the top sales associates in the southwest region for a store that sold overpriced white and black clothes for women. They paid by the hour, but they also offered commission on big sales. I thought I would be bad at the job, but the middle-aged clientele trusted my judgment, and soon I was spending hours waiting just outside the dressing rooms—*How's everything working out for you in there?* A woman would emerge in a billowy blouse that was just perfect for the cruise she was about to embark on, and soon I would have convinced her to buy twelve other things that went with the blouse, and then she'd be spending a thousand bucks.

I thought the job would feel sleazy, but I loved being in a store full of women, and most of them were using their husband's credit card anyway. However, the store moved from being down the street from me to the mall all the way on the other side of town. I hated working in the mall, with the smell of pretzels wafting in from the food court, and the store was so big that no one could track who was buying what, so I stopped making commission. People waddled in drinking soda and asking, *What's the deal with the black and white?* and I knew I had to quit.

At my American Apparel interview, I wore my black span-dex turtleneck dress—it was too hot to wear that day, but it was the only American Apparel I owned, and I knew my body looked good in it. The woman interviewing me had come from Los Angeles to help set up the store—she was gor-geous and competent and effortlessly cool. I don't remem-ber what kinds of questions she asked, but I remember it all seemed like a formality, as if the answers didn't really matter. She then asked if she could take a photo of me, making a big deal out of the fact that it was only so she could *remember me later*, since she was interviewing so many people. I agreed and posed in my dress, careful not to smile too much.

The next week, she called to tell me I was hired and asked me to come in for the store's first meeting. I think the rest of the new employees realized what I realized at exactly the same time, but no one dared say it out loud: we all fit an archetype. There was a blonde, a redhead, a brunette, an Asian, a Mexican, a half-black guy with an Afro, a gay guy, a curvy girl, a short girl, a six-foot-two-inch-tall girl. It was the strangest thing, the way no one ever addressed this directly. Of course we had been hired for our skill and abil-ity, we wanted to think. When the local newspaper came to photograph us modeling the clothes, it became pretty obvious what was going on. But to point it out would mean that we weren't grateful: the only people who com-plained were the people who didn't get hired. We were the good-looking ones, the cool ones, the ones who were paid almost twice as much as the Urban Outfitters employees across the street. We must have deserved it, we thought.

The atmosphere was lax: the store was always busy, but we never really rushed, and at night we took turns sipping rum and Cokes in the back room. We played music at a volume unbearable to adults—any parents who accompanied their daughters or sons would just sit outside until it was time to check out. One time I worked the register while a dad paid $200 for his daughter's new spandex bodysuits and thigh-high socks while Peaches's "Fuck the Pain Away" played. One time I was so helpful that a guy posted a Craigslist Missed Connections ad about me that said, *You were the angel in sea-green corduroy shorts.*

We drank in the back as a kind of pre-game move—there was always a house party somewhere. One night the blond employee, Lindsay, and I rode our bikes to the front yard of someone's house and never made it inside. I spotted my ex-boyfriend, who had broken up with me a few months prior (said he didn't love me, then said he did, then changed his mind again)—he was in the yard talking to some girl, so I turned to kiss Lindsay. This attracted two guys who had just moved from Portland, or maybe they moved to Portland later, I don't remember, but their personalities relied on their fixed-gear bikes. I didn't understand how a bike without brakes could be an identity, but they wore cycling hats with the fronts turned upward, and they always had their jeans rolled up on the right side so as not to interfere with their gears. They looked foolish, but they had faces like actors. And here they were, and so were we.

First I kissed the tall one while Lindsay kissed the short one. Then I kissed the short one while Lindsay kissed the tall one. Then the boys kissed each other, which was thrilling because everyone was always worried about being gay, even then. I could feel my ex-boyfriend watching me, thinking maybe I wasn't a virgin anymore, but who could be sure. We just went around kissing in a foursome, and we weren't even sitting—we were just standing there in a square like idiots, reminding me of the time my parents drove my sister and me to Four Corners, where you can touch Arizona, Utah, Colorado, and Nevada all at once.

For a Halloween party, I tucked *To Kill a Mockingbird* into a vintage fur coat and called it Harper Lee, and my best gay friend already looked like Truman Capote, so off we went into the night. The man I loved was there—no costume. Why hadn't I thought of that?

How lovely to be young enough not to know any better. I fell in love with anyone with a scar on their face.

I romanticize the desert because there's so much quiet, so much empty space. It feels as if anything could happen there, that I could meet anyone, that a coyote could emerge from behind a saguaro and wear sheep's clothing and I could fall for it and I could be happy.

Once, I awoke in the middle of the night, sensing something in the backyard but not hearing anything. I opened the second-floor window and listened—still nothing. *Come back to bed; you're dreaming*, my man said. In the morning, the backyard fence gate was open, and his bike was gone.

Years later, I awoke in the middle of the night next to another man and announced, *I'm dreaming of you, even now.* I couldn't wait until the morning to tell him—I wanted him to know that I never stopped dreaming about him, not even when I managed to capture his attention the way I'd wanted to. When I told him about all the detailed dreams I'd had, it was as if I was telling him about a life we'd already lived together—the prequel to the novel of the one night we had. That night, there was a big metal bowl on the steps leading to his front door, and when I asked about it, he said, *I don't know where it came from, but now I want to see if something will appear inside it.*

But even when he was holding me, I wanted the dream version of him. Something didn't match up.

I sometimes have phrases that won't get out of my head until I write them down. Here's one: *You were in my dream but not in my life.*

When I run on a treadmill, I have to imagine a future version of myself that kept running, the version of myself that decided to endure, to suck it up, to dream of a possible outcome.

The years back when I tried to put a price on myself: that wasn't so long ago, was it?

I like walking into the unknown the way I spend money: with my eyes closed.

With my eyes closed, I heard him say, *I don't love you anymore*. The man whose bicycle was stolen but wouldn't believe me—now he didn't love me, either. I could hear the words but I couldn't quite access them, couldn't quite accept that it was me living my life at that moment. Surely he was telling this to someone else, surely we would be together forever, the way we'd talked about. This was before I needed passion and wildness and to be on the verge of every emotion at once—I wanted safety and beauty, and he looked like Bob Dylan in the middle of the desert, and I thought that was what the love of my life could be.

Eventually I let out a laugh, the kind you might make in the middle of an emergency, just to hear yourself make a sound. Watching your life burn up—nothing left to do but ha. Ha. O. Kay. I was doing that slow-motion thing I do. I could feel myself delaying the inevitable: my life with him was over, a new life was about to start. When I walked through the door, five feet away, it would all begin, but I couldn't quite get there. I felt relief, even in that moment of agony—now I wouldn't have to marry him—but it was a story I'd told myself for so long that I wanted to delay the ending. Just one more minute.

*Are you okay?* he asked, after I don't know how long. *Yeah*, I said, and the word gave me enough strength to open the front door, push my bike out, and shut the door behind me. Two years. I was free.

I rode my bike up University Boulevard until I was out of breath. *Yeah.* We fell in love and fell out of it. That was the first time that had happened to me—it seemed impossible somehow. When I rode my bike alone at night in Tucson, it seemed as if I were the last person on earth. That's a wonderful feeling if you're a certain kind of person (I am).

Money needs us, depends on us to mint it, distribute it, exchange it, make it mean something, make it last. Dreams, on the other hand, don't need us at all. Some people have needed me, but the ones I wanted most didn't need anything or anyone.

My credit card debt gets higher and higher, seems to mean nothing. Maybe my monthly bill goes up $50. That's nothing compared to the thousands that went to black dresses, leather boots, cross-country flights, hotel rooms—all things that made me happy in the moment that I received them or spent time in them, all things that didn't last. But no amount of money can buy the love I've had. The way I loved was so wonderful that it seemed as if it must belong to another person. In those moments, I wanted only what I already had. But then it became something else.

The bite marks on my shoulder, his voice: *Good luck hiding that*, and I didn't care, because it was the only proof I didn't dream the whole thing up. He was real, his mouth was real, and it had marked me in a moment of rapture. It was over much more quickly than it began, but when I turned in the mirror the next day, he was still a little bit mine.

The performance of wealth can't work on me if I refuse to watch. If I cover my eyes and my heart at last, at last.

I was miserable when I was too poor to go to the doctor, too poor to buy more than one meal a day. But, at the same time, everything I bought was accompanied by a new promise, a new possible version of myself—me with a clean home, new clothes, a toned body, a respectable level of mental health. I remember buying five-inch leather wedge shoes for $300 because I fell in love with them on the Internet.

I copyedited an art magazine for free, for credit, for my résumé. It took me about twelve hours over the span of a few days. I was happy to do it, just to see my name on something (that old American urge). But then, the real payment: an invitation to the launch party at the Bowery Hotel. Finally, a reason to wear the five-inch leather wedges.

My feet hurt by the time I got there, but everyone was so fabulous, thank god I'd worn something besides my oversize James Dean T-shirt and black leggings. I saw one person I knew who worked at Acne Studios, and he introduced me to girls who worked at Opening Ceremony, but I already knew that because I'd seen their faces on the website, modeling the newest clothes.

I made my way to the bar to get the free cocktail that was made especially for the event. I saw Chloë Sevigny get one, and then Terry Richardson. By the time I got to the bar, the bartender told me they'd just run out of the free cocktail. I ordered a whiskey Coke and paid $15 and left a $1 tip and tried to make my drink last all night.

Someone I met introduced me to a painter who had recently appeared on a reality show. We flirted and he bought me another drink, and then I was drunk enough to spend the last of my cash on a third. I felt overwhelmed by the star power of the room, felt like a fake, so I welcomed his attention. An hour later, the party died down and we decided to walk back to the L together. As we walked up Third Avenue, we saw a sign for a fortune-teller—$5 FACE READING. He took my hand, and we walked in.

The fortune-teller looked at my black clothes and told me, *You are an artist and you are very sad.* I forget what she told the painter. It was a bad reading, but it was a strangely intimate act. The painter smiled at me as the fortune-teller looked for something to say. It was the kind of thing that bonds you forever. But in New York, you can make a friend like that, do something you've never done with anyone, have the best of intentions to see each other, and then disappear. We stood very close on the packed L train at two in the morning, and then he kissed me on the cheek when I got off at Lorimer Street, and I never saw him again—in person or on television.

*You were in my dream but not in my life.*

In my freshman year of college, I'd very often stay up all night every Sunday and go straight into Monday unslept.

It just didn't affect me; it was as if I didn't need sleep at all. My friend across the hall with the half-shaved head would come into my dorm room, and we'd do our homework together with all the lights on. Sometimes I'd go downstairs to get a sugar-free Red Bull from the vending machine, sometimes I'd just snack until morning. I never remember feeling the pain of not sleeping. I just remember the joy of being awake with my friend when everyone else had given up.

I attribute much of my personality to spending so much of my childhood on camping trips. My parents hated spending money on flying and hotel rooms, but they also just wanted to be outdoors in nature, not depending on anyone but themselves and their car and their tent and their gas stove. I've slept on one-inch foam pads on hard gravel soil, so now I can sleep anywhere. I've gone days without a real shower, so now I rarely feel dirty. I've spent days without spending money, so now I see how it can be done.

Floating down muddy rivers in a life vest with my feet first, I never knew what I was going to find. I used to howl like a coyote into the canyon just to hear what kind of noises I could make. I used to stay up late with my father and his friends under the moonlight just to see who drank the worm at the bottom of the tequila bottle.

I often have dreams in which I want to wake up but can't. I want to be alive but can't. I want to stop spending money but won't. I want to live my actual life, not my pretend life, but I just keep swimming through my mind, living on debt and hope.

How can I trust love if I can't ever truly touch it? I can touch a body, a face, a man, I can even feel a heart beating—what other proof of life is there? But physicality is not love. Bruises on a shoulder blade, a body on my body, a paycheck, a love letter—all innocent symptoms of a hungry disease. I starve myself until I can't. I love until I die.

I look to America for ideas and fall short. As a woman, I think I'm supposed to be fit but waifish, nurturing but alluring, innocent but independent, beautiful but without trying. I think I'm supposed to have children and be married and own a house by now, I think I'm supposed to make art a hobby instead of a reason to live—that would be best for money for security for buying things I think I'm supposed to want.

I once loved so hard I almost lost everything, including his life, including my own. Only then did I realize: perhaps love's physicality is death itself. I think I was taught that love, in its ideal form, is like a newborn baby: full of possibility, still warm from the heated privacy of the womb. But I think, at the end of my life, I won't see a figure cloaked in black velvet or a swirling void waiting to take me—I will see the face of love. It will be a recognizable light, the one that lived behind all those other faces I knew up close, the light I suspected but could never prove. When I see the face of love, I won't be afraid. I will see what I've been searching for all my life.

# Near Miss

Waiting is an enchantment: I have received *orders not to move.*

—Roland Barthes, *A Lover's Discourse*

*Do you wanna play?* Sam asked, using a jump rope to tie a butcher knife to his ceiling fan. His invented game had a name I no longer recall, but I looked at Julian, sitting on the couch, then back at Sam, standing barefoot on his coffee table, and I said, *Sure.*

It seemed like the type of thing that might occur more naturally at night, after a few drinks, but this was a Saturday afternoon, and the three of us hadn't even had coffee yet. Sam's house was alongside a dirt road in Tucson, near the University of Arizona, where I hoped to study journalism. I'd seen Sam sing at a basement show a few months prior and had fallen in love with the drummer, Julian, but called him something less suspicious—*my friend*. I'd borrowed my mother's minivan to drive the two hours from Phoenix to spend the day with them.

Sam tightened the knot around the butcher knife's handle as I took my seat next to Julian on the couch. *Are you ready?* Sam asked, and I said, *No*, but he pulled the fan's metal chain and rushed to his seat. *Keep your hands on the couch*, he said. *That's the rule.*

Arms at our sides, we watched as the knife picked up speed and the rope became stiff, pointing at us like an accusation. I averted my gaze from the knife to Julian, and, for a moment, I thought he might look back. The knife seemed like a kind of placeholder, an object standing in for the badness of the world, which had not yet reached us, not all the way. We brought it closer.

Schopenhauer wrote, *The scenes of our life resemble pictures in rough mosaic: they are ineffective from close up, and have to be viewed from a distance if they are to seem beautiful.* He argued that attaining a goal was beside the point—it's the ad interim which makes up our lives, that time leading up to the thing we thought we wanted.

The summer in between high school and college seemed disposable, and I woke up each day ready to waste it. I regarded college as the moment my life would finally begin. I wasn't ready, I wasn't smart enough, I wasn't in love enough, but time slowed as the knife made lap after lap pointed toward our foreheads. Julian had said we should make it the Best Summer Ever, and maybe this was that, I couldn't tell.

I expected Julian to love me back, I expected to *acquire* him, as in *the object of my affection*—a phrase I've always hated for its implication of ownership. It's a lie designed to give hope—someday, perhaps I would hold him in my hands and keep him forever. However, never *having* him might have been just as useful (Schopenhauer: *To attain something desired is to discover how vain it is*). I hoped for the end result, even though I couldn't define it, because I thought it was the only important thing. I'd been taught that all those days *before* I got what I wanted were hours to be hurried not valued.

We weren't sure how tightly the rope held the knife, if it would slip, when. I think it glittered each time it passed the sun in the window, but perhaps it only glitters now, when I try to see it again. Laughter, destruction, injury, love—listing them here, they appear distinct, as separate entities, but that's not right. The time in which we waited— that was the great equalizer, in which one consequence replaced another. Anything could happen, so, for a moment, everything did.

Then the fan's blades turned at top speed, and the knife slipped and darted toward my love—I mean my friend—and missed him by a few inches, stabbed the couch cushion instead. We gasped, said, *Oh my god*, and covered our mouths with our hands. We couldn't stop laughing at how close we'd been.

I ached for so many things then, I thought I could feel my bones still growing some nights, the way I did when I was a child. I longed for the future as if it would arrive in a clearly labeled box just for me, as if I could open it in mid-air as it hurled itself toward my shoulder. I failed to value its obscurity then, and I'm still failing, even now.

The inevitability of the knife simplified everything: each anatomy was available to ruin, each law was breakable. That's what made the world so beautiful, so seemingly new within its impossible history. I forgot that sometimes.

# The New Love

You look away: the new love!

You look back,—the new love!

—Arthur Rimbaud, "To a Reason"

*I went to San Diego and I didn't tell anyone*

Only my boyfriend, Cody, and his friend with the Corolla knew where we were going—we didn't have maps or the right kind of phones, just a highway we thought looked right. San Diego was eight hours away, so we left Tucson in the afternoon and, by sunset, realized we'd gone the long way. The two-lane highway wound up steep khaki-colored mountains where the radio turned to static and our phones went useless. The sun met the asphalt that met our eyes as we curled around each unprotected cliff—one wrong turn and we'd know. I was in the backseat, gazing at Cody's head in front of me in the passenger seat. I saw the way hot air roared through his open window and then his hair and then mine and I thought that meant whatever happened to him also happened to me and that must mean we were bound.

The day before, I'd taken notes in a lecture hall for my Psychology 101 class. My teacher walked up and down the aisles with a hands-free pop star–style microphone that clipped to her ear and hovered just above her mouth. She discussed the power of suggestion—the phenomenon of students experiencing the symptoms they read about. *For example,* she said, referencing a chapter we'd read the week prior, *you're not actually depressed, you only think you are.*

She also taught us the term *peak experience*, which psychologist Abraham Maslow wrote about in his book *Toward a Psychology of Being.* While collecting data in 1968, Maslow prompted a group of students to write about their own experiences by saying: *I would like you to think of the most wonderful experience or experiences of your life: happiest moments, ecstatic moments, moments of rapture, perhaps from being in love, or from listening to music or suddenly "being hit" by a book or painting.* Symptoms include loss of judgment to time and space, feeling whole and harmonious, and complete mindfulness of the present moment without the influence of past or expected future experiences. Sitting in the lecture hall, I couldn't remember ever feeling that way.

Our friend in San Diego answered the door with a little green bird perched on his shoulder. Behind him, a group of people sat on the floor, smoking cigarettes. I watched the bird move from his shoulder to his shirt collar and then disappear under the fabric, and our friend said, *He likes the warmth of my armpit,* and then, *Let's go to Coronado Island.* We loaded up two cars full of people and went to see about the salt we'd been smelling.

The hotel for rich people sat there like a prop as we walked around it to get to the beach. I kept waiting for someone in uniform to come out and tell us to go home or be quiet, but no one did. We were left alone with the fog on the beach, and I didn't need to feel the cold water for myself—I sat in the sand, watching everyone else hurry toward it.

I've tried before to write about Cody emerging from the fog, but I always end up cutting it out. This time, maybe I can get it right: I think it was his shoulder that first cut through the haze and made him identifiable. I think loving him that year was one of the best things I ever did. I think, at first, he was just a shape, like a memory recalled too many times—each time, he was a new story with a different ending—but as he got closer, I think the lights from the hotel made his face glow and I felt as if I was seeing him for the very first time. *I think I'm having a peak experience,* I said, and he asked, *What's that?*

### I went to Los Angeles and I didn't tell anyone

Goodbyes bored and embarrassed me—I didn't make a show of the move, I just shipped a few boxes and moved in with someone from the Internet. I thought living on Sunset Boulevard seemed glamorous, but each morning I awoke to a new layer of black soot on the windowsill. My address ended with a fraction, my room was painted lime green, and my bed folded back into the wall like a lie. One day, my roommate bought a taxidermy wolf in a howling position, and when I encountered it for the first time, in the middle of the night, I thought I must be dreaming.

My friend got married in the Los Angeles River, which turned out to be just a concrete ditch with a stream—an afterthought—trickling through it. That day, my friend's therapist played the role of ordained minister and said, *The thing about him is he turns everything into art.* His wife wore a gold dress that glittered in the daylight. I wore a bow tie and met a man from New York who also wore a bow tie and that was enough for us to end up in my lime-green room together that night. When I turned to him, I saw the moon gave my bed a suggestion of fullness, gave that man a kind of halo.

I'd been trying to turn my life into art, but I wasn't sure what form it should take. I played guitar with half-callused fingers; I found a discarded headboard on the side of the road and tied a hundred rope knots around it. I rented a studio so I could feel like an artist, and that worked for a while. I taped parts of essays to the wall in order to liberate them from my hard drive—to see them as whole. Rearranging them felt good, throwing them away felt even better. I was getting closer to saving only the most rapturous moments of my life. I disposed of memories until everything served me.

*Isn't this where James Dean stood in that knife-fight scene?* the man from the wedding asked, and I said, *I think so.* We could see the entire city from the Griffith Observatory, but we still took the elevator to ascend one floor higher. In line for the telescope, he squeezed my arm in segments, up and down, until I asked him what he was doing and he said, *I want to understand this little arm.*

When we reached the front of the telescope line, an employee said the winds were too strong to see Jupiter clearly, but *look if you want*. We wanted. The crisp outline of the planet appeared, then faded.

My roommate asked to take my portrait in the living room. *Okay, now look out the window*, he said. I watched the neon sign at the hardware store light up as the sun went down. The traffic, ugly as ever, made its sweeping sounds. *Okay, now look back at me.*

I once wrote a birthday poem for the man in the fog. After I read it aloud, I could tell he didn't get it and maybe didn't even like it, but a year later, he calls, says he found it when he moved and *it is so beautiful now.*

When the sand gets in our eyes, we blame the shifting of the ground; we feel the world adding itself up. The old love was a meadow where deer approached if you stayed still long enough. The old love was a staring contest in which blinking meant you were still playing. The old love was a basket of fruit begging to be painted, and sometimes we did paint it.

## I went to Phoenix and I didn't tell anyone

I didn't want to see people in my hometown; I was tired of asking the same three questions and listening to three inevitable answers. I thought I could just see my family and that'd be it—I watched my little cousin watch my mother sew a clear vinyl square into a piece of red fabric before draping it over a card table. *See?* my mother said, pointing. *Now it's a house.*

My mother was always so gentle with me when I felt depressed—I'd have my blinds closed and lights out in the middle of the afternoon, weeping over some middle-school injustice—and she'd sit at my bedside, asking if I wanted to talk about it. Sometimes I did, but other times I really, really didn't. She'd always say I'd feel better if I talked about it, but I wasn't sure she could know that. I liked the intensity of emotion, even if it was bad, and that's how I am now, too. Talking it out or walking it off dissipates whatever I'm feeling, and soon after that, it's really gone.

When I was in third grade, my friend's mother was a judge with her own courtroom, so our Girl Scout troop went to see her in action. When she used the gavel, we wanted to cheer, but we knew enough to stay quiet. Our troop leader took us back outside when we were done and said, *See? You can be anything you want to be.* But we weren't looking at her. We were watching the handcuffed men step off the bus, we were making eye contact. One of the men stuck his tongue out, aimed his crotch at us, and thrust against the morning air. Another called out, *Don't end up like me, girls.* In straight-faced unison: *We won't.*

When we were sixteen and the moon looked full and my friend's friend with the sports car got his driver's license, he drove so fast I swore we would die. The driver stayed very quiet and still as he shifted from gear to gear, then, when he reached ninety-five on the fifty-five-mile-per-hour-limit freeway, he laughed and laughed in a way that told me we were certainly, definitely just about to die—he was taking us with him. The fuller the moon, the crazier we felt, the more alive we wanted to be. Somehow we survived. I arrived at my childhood home in the same body I left in, delivered by a boy who wanted to die but never did.

*You can't just keep running,* a teacher told me once. But in the new love, I'm pretty sure I can. I had my passport photo taken with a Polaroid film camera that shot two images simultaneously. In one photo, I'm looking at you—the other, away.

## I went to New York and I didn't tell anyone

I didn't tell my friends I was visiting, I didn't tell anyone I was in love. I slept in his bloodred room under black sheets and the pentagonal glass lantern where a candle burned. I was afraid of falling asleep in the middle of a fire—I kept so much unwritten. The more I wrote, the more my secrets felt like the only things that were truly mine.

I didn't tell anyone what kind of sex I'd had, not even the doctor at the urgent care facility I went to a week later once I'd realized what was wrong. Urinary tract, I knew, but I still had to pee in a cup to prove it. The doctor took one look and said, *That's* infected *infected*, as if I'd lived twice.

The concept of *getting something out of your system* implies the person is capable of learning from her mistakes. But what if she loves her mistakes more than her life? I long and long—my acting is an attempt to cancel something out. *There,*

I say, putting lipstick on a face. Now I know what that's like.

Peak—the height of Bear Mountain. And no, not even that—the highest point was in fact an observation tower on top. Up four flights of stairs, I could see over the mountains and through the clear day: the Manhattan skyline I'd left that morning.

I want to be a building that bends with the wind. I want to be designed that way. I *give*.

The loudest of voices are the ones heard, but what of the smallest one, strengthening? What of the orchid in the window, getting just enough light?

### *I went to the gallery on Thirty-Sixth Street and I didn't tell anyone*

A performance artist hired me and thirty other people to help with her show, which hadn't yet been announced—we were told to keep it quiet. Our training involved eight hours of concentration and endurance exercises. In the middle of the first day, we broke off into pairs and stood facing four feet from each other. We stood in place for thirty minutes, but after ten of looking into my partner's eyes, I saw her face transform into a monstrous version of itself. She'd started childlike—rosy and dimpled—but then her skin turned tough and gray, resembling that of a blond rhinoceros, and then she was weeping onto the butcher paper we

stood upon. I could hear the wet drops hitting the paper
and expanding, but I didn't look down. I kept my eyes on
her eyes, trying to give her my strength, which felt unend-
ing for some reason. I thought maybe I'd found the one
thing I was truly good at: remaining motionless while someone else cried. A few minutes before the timer stopped, she
collapsed and steadied herself on the floor. I thought maybe
we were bonded forever, but we didn't speak that day, and
then I never saw her again.

Another exercise consisted of sitting and gazing at a white
wall. To my surprise, it was more difficult than the standing exercise. After just a few minutes, I saw colorful lights
flickering, and then I saw my spine represented as a hairline
crack in the paint—I saw bone, joint, marrow, fluid, cell. I saw
my whole life in little jars of heat, stacked on top of each
other. When I heard someone say, *Time's up*, I realized I'd
been crying this time.

Who could blame me for seeing only what I wanted to
see? Who could accuse me of anything? I loved everything
that didn't love me back; it was the easiest thing in the world.
Back then, I believed in change. I believed scaffolding was
the same thing as structure. I thought I could build it.

When the show opened, it was my job to blindfold visitors,
place noise-canceling headphones over their ears, and guide
them slowly into a large room they hadn't seen. The idea
was that the room would generate its own energy based on
whoever was inside. People stood still, paced around the

perimeter of the room, kissed, fell asleep, stayed ten minutes, stayed five hours. Sometimes they accidentally tried to walk through the exit—an open doorway—and it was my job to guide them back into the room without startling them. In my journal I wrote, *I'm paid to be a ghost.*

The old love was a bullet in the arm outside of a hospital—not ideal, also not deadly. It didn't mean our enemies didn't exist, that our wounds would heal any differently, that we'd see our lives flash, that we'd have some sort of epiphany. There was no guarantee, only possibility, which I may have loved more than my life anyway. But now, the new love is lying on the sidewalk, waiting for someone to carry it inside.

### *I went to the apartment by Central Park and I didn't tell anyone*

When he and I drank enough, each moment seemed like its own entity—I acknowledged the past as feasible, but I didn't see myself as *accumulating*. With this man who was not my boyfriend, I felt new, just born, and we slapped each other like doctors reminding themselves to breathe. He lifted his cup to his lips, and I asked, *Are you trying to send me a message?* One glassy look, then home.

When he loosened the tie from his neck, bound my hands together behind my back, said, *I'm not done with you yet*, I felt as if I were dreaming. And if I were dreaming, then maybe I could wake up. Maybe I could keep making decisions outside of this one. If I were dreaming, then this was just a phase.

If I were dreaming, then I could tell my boyfriend all about it, we could laugh later. Why was I laughing, then?

I laughed because no one knew where I was, which meant I was free. I never felt that way.

Clean like evidence, sealed off like a jury, I'd like to be a court document—available by request. I will pour myself into boxes, I will be released. Someday.

I'll say your name fully and often, the way they do in movies. You'll hear the shape of my mouth summoning you, singled out at last—you'll like it. I'll meet you at the barstools and you'll touch my hair and I'll take home everything you say. Don't you know you can't trust a writer? She'll see a cigarette and call it a house fire. She'll take a suggestion and turn it into a crime scene. She'll wrap herself up in caution tape. She'll write you down.

No one can make me face myself, no one can force me to confess. It's so easy to identify the right choice, but so difficult to choose wisely when I feel my life might last forever. Tonight I'm someone else, I'm using abandonment as a reward for work. I saw a man emerge from the fog as if he were born from it, and I thought, *This is a peak experience*, because I knew it was about to end.

The old love was broken windows with apple pies cooling on the sill. The old love was a desert island with white sand drifting upward like smoke when I waved to the rescue plane. The old love was a theater with its birth year carved in stone above the entrance. *You can't take a photo of the stage*, the usher warned, and the woman in the second row said, *I'm taking a picture of myself?* She said it like that, with a question mark at the end, a maybe. The new love is half human, half stage—we perform until we get it right. The new love is an incision where no one can see it, a bed folding into itself. The new love is a careless archive, just put it somewhere and hurry up would you.

# The End of Longing

I met a woman who drew illustrations of the products she wanted instead of buying them. Her wall was filled with silhouettes of designer handbags and big-screen televisions. The black-and-white drawings satisfied her, but looking at the wall made me want things I never knew I wanted.

◆

I've had enemies so intense that it felt romantic, so mutual it felt like love.

◆

*The truth is I don't care what anyone thinks*, I said to him over lunch. *That's noble*, he said, not believing me. *I think it's true*, I said. *I want it to be true*. Sometimes honesty requires three attempts.

◆

I once saw a magic show so convincing that I refused to acknowledge the possibility of illusion. I've done that with love ever since.

◆

Looking at the photo he took of me with my face half-lit against the brick building, my boyfriend said, *When I make a movie, I want the whole thing to look like this.*

◆

My friend and I went to see the movie about women in New York. The plot reminded me of my life, and I loved it. The plot reminded my friend of her life, and she hated it. *I think I identified with the wrong character*, she said.

◆

Old letters are not proof of love, but they are proof that we were aimed at, even reached for.

◆

He said, *Everyone just wants to be looked at*, and turned away from me to face the window.

◆

It took me years to realize silence could be an insult and was actually the worst insult. No one I'd loved had inflicted it on me.

◆

All characters appearing in this work are you. Any resemblance to real persons, living or dead, is purely you.

◆

My friend with the half-shaved head was like power in its most essential form—simply being near her made me bold. When it rained, she'd stand in the backyard and hold her arms out and face the sky—that's how alive she was. I loved her dirty Vans and her academic probation and the way everyone cheered like in a sitcom when she once rode her bike straight into the living room of a house party. I can't bear to think of her now, out in the world, getting older like a human.

◆

The day I decided I was more miserable than ever, my boss said, *You know what I like about you, Chelsea? Nothing is ever wrong.*

◆

All this technology and no app to quell the disappointment of getting what you want.

◆

The desire I feel is somehow *not earthly*—it's otherworldly, as in, I long for the *other*, for the life I could have led, there, or that one, there.

◆

What's the point of longing? To continue.

◆

For our high-school graduation party, our school hired a hypnotist. My best friend volunteered herself, went onstage, and fell asleep, and then he had her dancing and singing Backstreet Boys songs. When she woke up again, she walked back to her seat, and I tried to tell her what she'd done while she was out, but she said she was awake the whole time. *It was easier to just do what he wanted me to do,* she said, and I knew what she meant.

◆

Suffering feels religious if you do it right.

◆

Tending to everything and completing nothing—that's one way to postpone death. Art, too.

◆

The only time I ever got into a car accident was when I thought the light had changed but I was mistaken—I was still looking at the photos I'd just had developed and I drove into the car in front of me. This is my autobiography.

◆

I spent so much money on my education that I can't stop talking about how helpful it's been. I hate wasting money that much.

◆

*Rival* is often too generous a word.

◆

Each time I lie, I surprise myself a little less. And then I really shock myself. Then I forget.

◆

A man told me recently he was mystified by my *blind respect for masculinity.* I'd never thought of it that way. Even that moment—him pointing it out to me—impressed me so much that I realized maybe I did have a problem.

◆

*Show me the best thing you've ever seen*, I said, and he opened his Internet browser.

◆

When you're young, everyone's an artist. But it's a game of endurance, a fight against addiction, children, comfort, stasis, health insurance, home ownership. People drop off one by one. No one ever tells you that.

◆

My version of *cellar door* is *I desire a cauliflower ear*.

◆

The most mysterious love to me, now, is the love that I know has changed me but that I no longer remember. I think, *I must have been a different person to accept love in that awful form*, but I can't quite grasp the details. It's like trying to remember things from someone else's life—impossible. I can only see myself now, and even then, barely.

◆

Replacing hesitation with audacity is helpful for nearly everything.

◆

The assignment was to draw ourselves as comic-book heroes. One girl said, *I'll put a tree on my head, and a hawk on my tree-head branches, and then I'll win the war.*

♦

I'd only known her a few hours before she told me a secret she'd never even told her mother. We'd spent the day buying clothes, calling boys, taking funny pictures, and waiting until the lights were off to actually talk. *That step-father?* I pointed to the door.

♦

A theory my friend has: sleepovers are where girls learn to wake up in love. *Remember when we knew our friends' bodies as well as our own?*

♦

I put my hand on the shoulder of my high school boy-friend when I saw him twelve years later. It was my turn to startle him.

♦

A lie emerges from the lake, evolving, standing on two feet now. I let it live.

♦

When my heart was broken for the first time, my friend said, *Maybe this will be good for your art*, and he was right.

♦

What's the end of longing? More longing.

◆

I documented everything, tracking each movement. *Today, I wrote, he closed his eyes when I talked.* I ran at each red flag, a grunting bull alone in the ring. A red light on my phone, and soon he was under me. One sad breath, and *Do you miss me like I miss you?*

◆

I don't want to *be with* you, I want to *become* you.

◆

He only wants to make things so that people adore him. I say that attention is beside the point, making beautiful things should be the only goal, but then I remember how badly I want him to adore me.

◆

A poem is a way of talking to the person you're not supposed to talk to anymore.

◆

*Don't be sad*, he said. *It's not tomorrow yet.*

◆

My friends who are cruelest to the world are kindest to me.

◆

*Do you remember what we talked about last night?* one man asked me. I tried to bring myself back to that room, so many drinks later. I had a feeling we'd admitted something to each other. *No*, I said, *I don't remember*, and I didn't ask him for details. If there was tenderness that night, now it belongs to him.

♦

I hope for the discovery of more truth, but not the whole truth.

♦

*You look like you're suffering*, a man I'd just met said, and I said, *I'm the human embodiment of the opposite of suffering.*

♦

A cloud came to cover the moon in the final stages of the eclipse. I didn't see the ending, but I still understand the story.

# Pity the Animal

I was sitting on the rooftop of my apartment building in May, waiting for July's fireworks. I was cleaning high-rise condos in Manhattan, teaching fourth grade in Queens, eating wheat-bread-and-American-cheese sandwiches that the government delivered to the school. I was writing everything down as if I knew what I was seeing. I was pretending to be a neutral observer, but I kept trying to override my heartbreak with poignancy. It was almost working.

I missed the structure of school, syllabus handouts guiding my hours. I always thought I wanted to be free, but as soon as I was free, I longed to be corralled, guided. I couldn't get a job as a journalist, so I got jobs that had nothing to do with writing. My friend told me I could have any man I wanted, so I maneuvered through the city not having any of them.

The invitation said: *Wear your costume*, a Halloween barbecue in May. I went dressed as my Freudian id. A man approached me, said, *I'm a burglar, too*, and pointed at his mask, the same one I wore. Later, a couple invited him to a sex party, said they needed someone sober to drive their SUV. He said, *You have to come with me*. It felt easy being told what to do. I assigned myself to him like a grade.

Still wearing his bandit mask, the man opened the passenger door to the car. I stepped in, noticed a bottle of lube on the dashboard. The couple who owned the car began making out in the backseat. They both wore studded dog collars, but the woman kept grabbing the man's collar and saying, *Motherfucker. Motherfucker.* As we drove over the Williamsburg Bridge, I realized I wanted the burglar to touch my thigh, but he kept both hands on the wheel. When we got to the building in the Financial District, the sun was rising, and the bouncers said we were too late. I wore my mask on the subway home.

It was the summer Marina Abramović sat in a chair at the Museum of Modern Art for eight hours every day. Visitors who were willing to wait in line for hours or days could sit across from her for however long they wanted. When I visited, I observed from the sidelines. I'd never seen anything like it. I found her beauty most hypnotizing before the fact of her stamina registered.

An e-mail to my friend in Oregon: *Do you know who Marina Abramović is? She's doing this performance piece at MoMA where you can sit in front of her. Some people are hogging their turn, they sit there all day with her. One woman took her clothes off, another woman wore the same floor-length blue dress as Marina. I have this urge to sit with her and cry just to see if I can.*

I feared her gaze—she made a person feel like the only one in the room. I wanted to feel fractional.

This well-documented, now-famous performance was titled *The Artist Is Present*. Each time I paid my museum admission, I was paying to see her body.

In June, I found a way to get paid for my body—I worked as a model for a men's clothing ad. I was not the focus of the photo, but I sat on a lawn chair in the background, reading a paperback copy of *Catcher in the Rye*. That morning, a large man had teased my hair into a lion's mane, smoothed it into a housewife bouffant, then curled the ends. As he slipped each curl out of the iron's round barrel, he held it in his hand like a baby bird, blowing on the hair until it cooled. *Doesn't that hurt your hand?* I asked. He looked at me in the mirror and said, *No, baby, I'm a man.*

The stylist, a sweaty woman in red stilettos, fretted over the clothes not fitting me. I was a size two, the same size as when they hired me the week prior, but all the clothes were a sample size zero. I stood beside the rack of clothes, naked except for the flesh-toned Victoria's Secret thong she'd given me that morning. I hadn't taken a photo all day. The stylist found a dress that was too big for me and sewed me into the dress. *Now just don't move or go to the bathroom.*

No one ate the colorful buffet, no one let me stand next to the roof's edge. Then, at the end of the day, the photographer told me to sit on the edge and arch my back. Two weeks later, I got a check in the mail for $800.

I kept going back to MoMA to look at Marina Abramović. I felt closer to her, closer to sitting in front of her, though I did not wait in line. Watching her meant I didn't have to watch myself, didn't have to face anything besides the museum. My body was simple. I missed modeling when I didn't get more jobs.

My financial situation wasn't dire—bills got paid—but I started considering the possibility of commodifying my body. People spoke of it as if it were detached from me, and perhaps that was true in a way. It trailed behind me like a valuable shadow.

I kept hearing the phrase *That's the price you pay*—for living in New York, for dressing the way you do, for focusing on art. What would happen if I stopped paying the price? What if someone assigned a price to me? What if someone else paid that price?

Sick of balancing multiple roles, some days I wanted to be less human.

Sylvia Plath quoting her pen pal Eddie Cohen in her journal: *Fifteen thousand years . . . of what? We're still nothing but animals.*

If I'm sold as an object, then I'm no longer a threat. My mind spoken for, contained, no one waiting for proof, my body no longer my own. But why would I long for something that happens so effortlessly to less fortunate girls, less middle-class girls, less white girls?

Fear breeds fantasy, and I feared my mind would be forgotten.

*I'm responsible*, says Nana the prostitute in Jean-Luc Godard's *Vivre sa vie*. And responsibility was the thing I wanted to be rid of—I had a desire to watch the world, admire it from a balcony that held no authority.

From *Selling Service with the Goods*, a 1921 book about constructing window displays: *Women, as a rule, are highly responsive to the delicate, softer tones and tints which are so necessary in portraying a domestic product in colors. The man, as a rule, prefers something more than a delicate violet background as the color base for a display advertising a shot gun. Such a display must be strong—perhaps a little rough—in treatment.*

I was the lilac mannequin, displaying myself without words. I was on the rack, waiting to be touched.

It seemed logical to continue on the conflict-free route I'd arrived at—how lucky I was, always deciding who reached for me. But I could see my own limits, and I wanted to run toward them with a price placed upon me like a blanket.

I didn't need to reduce myself to an object in order to be sold. I needed only to be animal.

From Joseph Delmont's 1931 book, *Catching Wild Beasts Alive*: *Out in the forest, fields, jungle, and plains: Everywhere where the animal is still at liberty and is little harassed by men, its real behavior can be observed, and then men can learn much, for there the animals are sound, their natural instincts are displayed, and they provide an example for us.*

Example:

$8 per hour: When I worked at the copy and printing place, a man asked me to make copies of dollar bills for him. I said no, there was a rule against that. But he assured me he was kidding. He said, *I just wanted to see your face*, so I showed it to him.

$10 per hour: At American Apparel, they gave everyone a free swimsuit in exchange for wearing it to work. They didn't force anyone to take the swimsuits, but everyone took them. At first I felt embarrassed of the black bikini, but after an hour, I worked alongside capitalism's heartbeat; I could sense a faceless man benefiting from my shape. And in fact, he wasn't faceless at all—I knew who I sold myself for. I signed up for that.

$120 for six hours: I served drinks at a cocktail party selling expensive carafes. After I served merlot to the same man seven times, he cornered me near the coats, told me he was vice president of an airline, told me about the weather in Houston, because he was too afraid to ask what he wanted to ask. I held the carafe between us like collateral, said, *I better get back to work*. He said, *What a dutiful little thing*.

$8 per hour: The Russian man asked me to come into his office, his heavy accent listing his own accomplishments instead of interviewing me about the filing job. He said a man was outside right now, painting his Corvette. *What color?* I asked. *No, he is making painting on canvas of my*

*Corvette.* It was difficult to smile. *You don't mind if I make massage?* At first I thought he was asking to touch me, but he picked up the phone and began making an appointment. He put the phone on speaker and looked into my eyes as he asked the receptionist for the youngest masseuse they had. My gaze was quiet but direct, my limbs motionless. I realized I wanted to pass his test just because I could.

In *Selling Service with the Goods,* businessmen claim genius is nothing more than the ability to "take pains" with the job in hand.

In Marina Abramović's 1974 performance *Rhythm 0,* she put seventy-two objects on a table and allowed the gallery audience to use the objects on her for six hours. Someone cut her shirt off. Someone put rose petals on her nipples. A man loaded the single bullet into the pistol and pressed it against her neck. In her performance proposal, she wrote, *I am the object. During this period I take full responsibility.*

In her *Role Exchange* performance the following year, a prostitute in Amsterdam replaced Marina at her gallery opening, and Marina replaced the prostitute in her red-light district window. The performance proposal stated: *We both take total responsibility for our roles.*

Taking responsibility is another way of forgiving someone else for their possible actions. Marina doesn't *have* responsibility, she *takes* it before reducing herself to a body.

More advice from *Selling Service*: *The trick is to attract atten-tion and to hold by force or interest until the decision to buy has been created.*

The closest I came to selling myself as an object was display-ing myself on a website called Seeking Arrangement. The website advertises itself as *the elite sugar daddy dating site for those seeking mutually beneficial arrangements.* It is, quite clearly, a loophole for prostitution.

When I made my profile, I chose the *Negotiable* price cate-gory. After a week on the website, I got so many responses that I changed my price to *$5,000 to $10,000 monthly.* Credi-ble responses were rare, but I still received a thrill with every new message. I watched a *Dr. Phil* episode on YouTube about women who paid for entire homes with money they'd made on Seeking Arrangement.

I tried to join WhatsYourPrice.com, a site where men make specific monetary offers to take women out on dates, but my profile kept getting rejected. The website e-mailed me with one request: *Be less obvious.* Seeking Arrangement approved my profile, which said, *I deserve to get paid.*

An e-mail from my friend in Oregon: *Did you cry in front of the artist yet?*

A man sent me a photo of himself next to a Lamborghini and offered me a thousand dollars "per meet." I sent him a photo of myself wearing lingerie. *What's your name?* he wanted to know.

What I know: my middle name is Rose; I once trespassed through a rose garden because it was the fastest route home; my mother named me after her best friend. What I don't know: what it's like to fuck a stranger; why I once told a man my first name was Rose; why, when he called me that name, it felt like trespassing.

E-mail correspondence with a Los Angeles "business executive" who called himself Storm on Seeking Arrangement:

> Storm: Wow, okay. You are already a dangerous temptation. How in the course of one e-mail have you already made my cock rock hard? Here I am, trying to concentrate on these contracts, and now I'm so distracted. I'll show you. Can I ask: would you be, well, open-minded if we meet?
>
> Rose: Sure, what do you have in mind? We also haven't discussed how much you're going to pay me.
>
> Storm: Well, I have some pretty naughty fantasies. I was thinking $800.
>
> Rose: What would you do to me? My price is $1,000.
>
> Storm: You want all the gory details, or just in general? Ha.

Rose: Tell me what you want.

Storm: Well, I was having this dirty fantasy about
you on your knees, in pretty white panties,
my fingers twisted into your hair, pulling
your head back hard, kissing and biting your
neck, spanking and grabbing your ass, rub-
bing your pussy through your panties and
feeling you get soaking wet through the fabric; then tearing two holes in your panties so
I can lick and suck and finger your ass and
pussy; and then, well, fuck you in your ass
and pussy with my thick hard cock through
the holes in your panties . . . That's the fantasy. Damn, I'm so turned on again. And I
have to leave soon to go to this banquet.

From *Selling Service with the Goods*: *What the consumer sees,
open before him or in operation, he is apt to desire to examine more
closely—to test its uses.*

In Los Angeles, my friends spotted a hole near the bottom
of the wall along Exposition Boulevard. It was the Fourth
of July when we crawled through the broken bricks and
turned the rose garden into a shortcut. We touched the petals, but all we could smell were the fireworks reaching
their dark ends above us. No one guarded the roses. We kept
walking.

What if I walked into a hotel room? The gray-haired
man has done this before. He tells me to undress, get

on my knees, look into his eyes. A gold condom wrapper falls to the carpet like a ticket stub. He holds me by my limbs, as if that's where my responsibility grows. What if he enters my ass? What if I agree to do anything for that dull green stack on the nightstand? What if the choice is no longer mine?

Marina Abramović: *It's because I want to be a whore. My mother was calling me so many times a whore.*

I'm presented to the world, watched, and participation is the key to a room I think I could enter. I could be led there.

It must feel good to have that much money. It must feel patriotic to hold it. I must be crazy to let a man do that. He must hold me down and make me take it. The hotel must be an island where no one can hear me. I must get lost in that place.

If my job is to display myself in a window, then I will lure men inside. They will ask questions about my use. I'll get off on my functions.

Joseph Delmont, hunter: *As a rule, an adventurer is considered equivalent to a criminal. This is an utterly false idea.*

I never went through with it. There were so many details to work out; the negotiation became a dominance I despised. Take me to a room, take advantage of me—simple—but it didn't take long to realize my mind was the only place

I could be wholly submissive. I wanted to receive money for my body the same way young girls pack up their belongings but never run away. The difference was men were telling me where to run, where they'd take me. I could choose any place in the world, any hotel in New York.

When I heard Marina Abramović had stopped sitting at MoMA, I felt relieved. I would no longer have to pretend I was planning to sit with her.

Nana in *Vivre sa vie: I shut my eyes—I'm responsible. I forget that I'm responsible but I am. I told you there's no escape.*

From a YouTube video called "GTA [Grand Theft Auto] 5 Take a Stripper Home, Have Sex with a Stripper (BOOBS) GTA V":

(Road map appears on screen.)

> *Hello everyone, this is your boy Joseph, and I hope you're having a fantastic day. And as you can see, we're playing GTA 5, and the goal of this video is to see how far can I go with the stripper. So as you can see, I have $231 and I'm Franklin . . . according to the game it's a Wednesday, so okay, let's do this.*

(Map zooms in to lower right, where a high-heel icon appears.)

> *So, the strip club, if you go to the map, it's this little high-heel thing . . .*

(Old Corvette speeds down city streets.)

*Oh, yeah, by the way, (inaudible) have a nice car just for fun, but I picked up this one. Last time I found the Lamborghini, but I crashed and died.*

(Car arrives at strip club. Franklin walks inside.)

*Here's the strip club. "Vanilla Unicorn," aw, yeah. So we walk in, there's the ATMs, shows you your money, you can walk in here, get drinks if you want, get a little bit faded before you get a lap dance or something, so you just walk down here, there's this girl dancing.*

(Franklin is standing in front of the stage as a stripper dances on a pole. He fails to turn before he walks and walks in place, facing the stage, then turns to the left.)

*So just click there, and I mean, she's dancing, you can toss a dollar . . . one dollar, or make it rain.*

(Franklin tosses four one-dollar bills.)

*Sweet. Just look around, look up. Oh, yeah, you work that pole, girl. (Laughs.) And now we're gonna go to, uh . . .*

(Stripper walks toward Franklin and starts dancing in front of him.)

*Ooh, yeah, get close, girl. She's all right from the face. Let's make it rain again on her.*

(Man offscreen says, *I'll lick your asshole 'til it shines!* Stripper walks up, says, *I missed you, Franklin!* Franklin walks away. Another stripper comes up, says, *Follow Infernus, I'll take care of you.*)

*All right, I like that ass, girl . . .*

(Infernus appears topless in a private room, motions for Franklin to sit in the chair. She's wearing a silver choker necklace, a black thong, and knee-high red boots.)

*Oh! Tit . . . uh . . . wow . . . boobs! Boobs!*

(Infernus shows her ass, and she has a huge purple bruise on her right side. She turns to show her bare breasts.)

*Oh my god, I didn't know this happened.* (Reading from instructions onscreen.) *"Touch and flirt with the dancer to increase her 'Like' meter. Make sure the bouncer doesn't see you touch her or you'll get thrown out."*

(Bouncer appears in the hallway, monitoring the private room.)

*"Press X to flirt . . ."*

(Franklin says, *Keep telling me how great I am.*)

*"Press* (inaudible) *to end dance" . . . No, I don't want to end dance. I guess I have to just keep telling her she's cute . . .*

(Franklin says, *Keep doin' what you doin'* . . . *I love your tattoos, baby, really cool.*)

*Wait, is the bouncer coming back? I can't tell.*

(Infernus says, *These tits are the best you'll ever see.*)

*I* . . . *I don't even know what to respond to that* . . . *Oh, is he gone? He's gone; touch her! Touch her! Oh, he's back.*

(Bouncer reappears. Franklin says, *Keep telling me how great I am.*)

*So when he goes away, we're gonna touch her* . . . *Let's make sure he doesn't watch us touch her* . . . *Oh my god* . . . *I think he left* . . . *Let's touch her!*

(Franklin reaches his right arm out, touches her hip, says, *Keep telling me how great I am.*)

*Those nipples are not even* . . . *that graphic.*

(Franklin says, *Okay, that's enough, bae.*)

*No! No! That's not enough! I want more!*

(Infernus gets off the chair and stands up.)

*Aww, is it over?*

As a twelve-year-old, I played a computer game called *Purple Moon* in which a wholesome red-haired avatar navigates middle school, making friends and getting good grades. The game had an accompanying website with a way to message other users. The site attracted young girls who played the game, so men also joined the site with girly usernames and talked to me about sex. I was not repelled by the messages; in fact, I loved them. I played along until their accounts got deleted by some larger censoring entity that I seemed exempt from. I remember being as explicit as the men were being. I was good at mirroring their voices back to them, so good that they often suspected I was a man as well. *God, you're dirty.*

That was the first time I expressed what I wanted, or what I imagined myself wanting.

I couldn't imagine holding a cock, but I suspected its ability to *take* me. Sex as kidnapping—the pleasure of being gone. I typed, *We're in a field. We're having sex in a field.*

Regarding window displays of household objects: *Women, in particular, like to see things as they look in use . . . A desire for merchandise is created by seeing it as it looks to others, in its natural surroundings, and as it will serve in actual use.*

The news reported proof of crows dropping nuts in the street so cars would do the cracking for them. I read ravens could look in a mirror and recognize a self. The birds evolved; I recognized myself in a new reflection.

A message from another man on Seeking Arrangement: *I know what you are. I know you keep it secret. I know you love being talked down to, called a whore, called a worthless piece of shit right before being slapped across the face. I know you dream about being raped, used like a whore should be, and I know you're scared to tell anyone.*

My money whispers small denominations in my ear. My money runs marathons.

Inside an old library book I requested from offsite storage, I found a scrap of paper with typewriter text that said, *Pity the animal that has no animal in it.*

Written inside another library book: *Mutilation noted.*

How much can a body endure? Almost everything.

When I still lived in Arizona, I sat down on a tattered futon at a house party, and my blond friend handed me a bottle of blue Gatorade. *There's vodka in it*, she said. She was the kind of woman who served drinks at other people's parties. The vodka gave strength to my desires, so all night we swam upstream in the blue water. Everyone watched.

I was the last person to leave the party. As I buttoned my coat, the host of the party touched his beard, laughed, and said, *No, no, no.* I wrapped my scarf around my neck, picked up my bike leaning against the living room wall, and walked toward the door. *Stay*, he said, and he wasn't asking.

He took my bike from my hands, placed it back against the wall, kissed my blue lips, pressed me onto the futon. He got completely naked; I had all my clothes on, even my boots. With my head against the wooden frame, he thrust himself into my mouth until he came, then fell asleep holding me in place. I stayed beside him for hours in the dark room, not sure how to get up.

Though he did force himself on me, the truth is I stayed at the party waiting for something to happen. Everyone at the party left, and still, nothing had happened. He wasn't a stranger—I knew he was a bad man, I'd known that for a long time. That's why I stayed.

I spent so much of my youth waiting for something to happen. Unsupervised, I had my choice of dark rooms. I knew which rooms were bad and I entered them anyway. It was a sort of power.

*When a colorful object is seen by the human eye, it is really not the color of the object which is seen, but the colors reflected from the object.*

I go to a party—I am responsible.

A woman becomes a girl becomes an animal becomes an object. Is there anywhere left to go?

As a young girl, I got up and walked to the bathroom during the Ringling Bros. circus. When I came out of the stall, I saw a reporter I recognized from television. She leaned against the sink, applied pink lipstick with a precision I admired. She noticed me and said, *Hi, sweetie*. When I returned to my seat, I watched a man lead tigers to their assigned positions.

I'm tired of the line that someone drew down the middle of me. He split me into halves and said, *Stay symmetrical or else*. Or else what? No answer, and yet I obeyed that command my whole life.

In March, I stood in a crowd at two in the morning waiting for elephants. The Ringling Bros. were scheduled to emerge from the Queens Midtown Tunnel, and I felt like a child standing there on Thirty-Fourth Street. The six beasts approached holding each other's tails with their trunks, a stifled yet efficient parade to Madison Square Garden. I took a photo of them walking in front of a Bank of America. I started running alongside the barricades to keep up.

On Seeking Arrangement, I exchanged messages with a handsome older actor who told me he had a German accent. I imagined it telling me what to do. A year later, I saw him in an online banking commercial. It was not a speaking role, but he pretended to work on his laptop in a café. The voiceover said, *You feel safe. But are you too safe?*

At a Yellowstone campsite entrance, the ranger warned my father of the recent grizzly bear sightings. My mother turned to look at my younger sister, who was terrified of bears. She kept her headphones on and eyes closed as we drove into the campsite. That night, in the yellow tent, I awoke to large, searching footsteps. *Did you hear him?* I asked my parents the next morning, and my sister began to cry.

*It is always wise to tie a bright colored ribbon around your bear's neck or on his leather collar so that thoughtless sportsmen, boys, and farmers of the neighborhood will recognize it as a pet and not run it through with a pitchfork or bullet.*

A friend once told me, *That top button isn't fooling anyone, you know.* A man once said, *As soon as I saw your top button, I knew you were a slut.* My top button: my protector, my signal.

A fire commands its audience. A flare in the middle of the road brings a man right to me.

At the Mid-Manhattan Library, I saw a girl I recognized from Arizona. When I went to school with her, she always had her head in a book as she walked, so it made sense to see her browsing the stacks. We had several classes together, but we were not friends, and I found myself walking to the library's exit so she wouldn't see me. In her, I recognized the meek reflection of someone I used to be. I walked away from that person.

*Under no temptation should a hunter's last shot be fired at a retreating beast.*

Human: to be *more than*. I pity anything stuck in one role.

While technicians prepared red, white, and blue explosives along the Hudson River, I snuck through a Brooklyn turnstile with my friend so we wouldn't be late for the party. The police were waiting for us on the other side. One cop said, *How'd you like to spend the Fourth of July in jail?*, which was stupid because we all knew girls like us were never punished, not really. We stuffed our $110 tickets into our back pockets and watched the fireworks from a famous singer's rooftop on the Lower East Side. I wanted to talk to the famous singer, but she kept gliding around on roller skates. I didn't want to be the reason she stopped.

The man in the bandit mask kept going as I watched him pee at the party in May. I loved the way he unbuckled his belt, unzipped, and pulled his cock into his hands, proud, casual. He had his back to me, but I looked around him to watch. He asked, *Wanna hold it?* and I did want to.

I wished his question was, *Wanna know what it's like to be the one who enters?* because I do, and I wish that knowledge was as simple as holding a man in my hands. I want to see my desire as a protrusion leading me into dark rooms. If I can't have that, then I can attempt to reduce myself to the most vulnerable object possible. Either I await instruction on how to be a dutiful thing or I am the explorer leading this ship or I am a piece of luggage holding other belongings. I take up barely any space at all.

It's true that I want what I can't have, but it was never my intention to please Freud. I'd like to feel satisfied with my own autonomy, but it seems like a job to experience something outside myself. It feels like a respected field. What would Freud say if I inspected his lap? What did Freud ever hunt?

In Joseph Delmont's book about trapping animals, he wrote: *The true adventurer always has an object in his wanderings.*

There is an island where former versions of myself gallop around on all fours. Untouched, the island populates itself; the versions share what they've learned. They never run out of things to talk about by the fire that the latest version knows how to start. If Joseph Delmont came to the island intending to trap a tiger, he might find one. The version might go willingly, without a fight. The island feeds off itself. I wait to be discovered.

So circle me like the prey I'm dressed as, erase my penciled-in boundary, pay me for the privilege. If I wave a flag of your face long enough, I can forget my own.

# The Id Speaks, Mid-Decision

Today was all sunshine and car crashes but I didn't let either stop me, not even when they closed all the lanes on the I-10 in the middle of the desert and swept the cars off the road like leftovers, five lanes into one, and then into a detour that took two hours to go twenty miles, I could see the freeway up ahead and it was so, so clear, the way it had been for me the whole ride up, nothing but me and my indignation, I Would Go The Whole Way Alone, I checked my phone and learned that a tour bus crashed into a semi-trailer and 13 people died and 31 people were injured and I thought of the mirrored numbers before I thought of how many lives were lost, one three three one one three three one, the bus crunched accordion style, dramatic, me and the drivers of lesser vehicles—we considered the horror of the accident, and we considered our lives, too, but mostly that we had been inconvenienced, of course we deserved our luck and our willingness to stay alive—we were the kinds of cars that became so unrecognizable we had words like *totaled* assigned to us, when we got in accidents we were completely wasted, totally done, but right now I was just going to be so, so late, I had to pee and I was hungry, it took me forever to even get to the gas station two miles up, as I crawled along Indian Canyon Drive I thought of the other car crash I had passed three hours prior, the one with the truck that you might call *totaled*, it was so done it had to be attached to another truck in order to move, I'm like that sometimes, I chain myself to you and call it a day, I touch the back of your head and call it a nightmare,

I trail one scent and call it two lives, but when I passed that
first crash, I thought, *Like a woman*, that is, the truck reminded
me of a woman, her capacity to be ruined, I thought I was
strong, I thought I could drive myself anywhere, and I did,
sometimes just to follow through on something, what did
I ever think I was doing, wherever was I, the truck didn't
remind me of myself because no one knows what their specific ruin will look like until it arrives, I was on the preci-
pice but not quite there, I was driving so far to be here with
you, I was on the verge of ruin which is not the same as ruin
unless you get caught, I never knew it could be like this,
total muse, I never knew your face could change in the light
of my indignation, my insistence that I love you and that you
love me, that you're worth the disaster that gets a little bigger each day I choose to continue, and make no mistake:
each day is a new choice, a new betrayal, a new life I lead
outside of the one I already live, I am given two options and
I choose both, both, one three three one, it was just one of
those days that seems as if something is about to go wrong,
the lightning and then the thunder like math, if we got in
our own car crash then what, what would I even say to anyone, what if I got in a car crash and kept it a secret, what if
I lived a life and held it for myself like your face when we fuck,
but today I opened my eyes halfway and saw green ones
like mine, brown-black hair and freckles and a big nose like
mine, I saw the mouth open like *O* like the holy part of a
poem like the way I do when I feel something about to happen
to my body, and I was feeling that, seeing that, I was seeing
myself, I decided, I was facing myself at last, I looked terrible wide open like that like I was trying to make the entire

world fall in, wasn't I discerning at all, wasn't I picky, wasn't I looking in the right direction ever, I felt so far gone, so totally the right truck on the wrong road, all it takes is one second of distraction, I was afraid I would crash and then I'd really have to see myself as the mistake that I am, crunched hood and airbags inflating to save me from myself, but then I stopped the car before it hit the car ahead of me with its brake lights shining and I was safe again, there was nothing to report, no omen, just the possibility of ruin, which is always present, which is what drew us to each other in the first place, how did we find each other in this world, who have I become, I see you and I see myself, everything I've kept, my omitted record like something to learn from, except I know the lesson already and I've decided to unlearn it each day, I love my tendencies and I hate being right, I love your voice when you sing other people's songs, I love the face I make when I want the world and now I can see it, I can see that I fuck myself over and over and over again, and that repetition is the only thing I reach for on this awful highway full of half-paved shoulders and reflective vests and orange cones guiding me to nowhere, and I see how I move according to each detour, and I see exactly how much time this one takes, and I see now it's impossible to stop.

# I'm Only a Thousand Miles Away

When my friend Alexis and I were in the sixth grade, my mother took us to a water park in Phoenix called Sunsplash. My mother sat in the shade, reading, while Alexis and I wandered around, going down the waterslides, swimming against the current in the wave pool, and, finally, floating on inner tubes on the Lazy River, a circle of water with a gentle current that looped us around the park.

Two boys our age paddled their way up to us. The more attractive one, TJ—tanned, with defined abs—began talking to Alexis and her buoyant tits, which were just as mysterious to me as they were to him. Her disproportionately large chest made her bold, and I hoped some of her boldness might make its way to me and my flat-chested boy body—no luck yet. For now, I was talking to the less attractive friend—Freddy, a pale, soft boy with a gentle demeanor. He sat up on his inner tube and showed me his love handles. I asked him to repeat the term, which I'd never heard, and he said, *You know, handles. For love.*

When it was time to go, we borrowed a pen from the corn dog stand and we all carved our phone numbers into napkins. When Freddy gave me his, I saw the dampness from his hand had smeared the numbers, but I could still read them. Alexis and I hid the napkins in our hands as my mother drove us home.

I hadn't liked Freddy that much in person, but on the phone, I was charmed by his jokes. The calls also gave us the chance to talk about our good-looking friends, who both impressed and terrified us. Last week, TJ's father drove TJ

forty-five minutes and dropped him off at Alexis's house
and they had made out in her room. The logistics of this
seemed impossible to Freddy and me, and yet we knew it
was the truth. Our friends were the kind of people who
made things happen, and we were the kind who waited for
other people's magic to touch us. Freddy and I pieced together
both sides of their stories until we'd imagined the event so
thoroughly that it became ours, too.

I liked the way the phone connected my voice to someone else's without a real commitment. It was casual, like
instant messaging—I'd let silence fill the line if I had nothing to say or if I wanted to think before continuing. My calls
could last hours, until my phone ran out of battery and
beeped and I had to quickly say goodbye before placing the
phone back in its lime-green holster on the wall next to
my bed.

My phone was made of translucent lime-green plastic,
and it brightened with a red LED light each time it rang. I
shared a phone line with our computer's dial-up modem, so
I could be either on the phone or on the Internet, but I had
to choose. After a few months, Freddy and I ran out of things
to talk about, since we knew our parents would never drive
forty-five minutes to drop us off at the other's house. We'd
never kiss, and our friends would likely never kiss again.
Eventually, the light stayed unlit.

Fan mail had been my primary mode of communication
with boys up until that point, passing notes to boys in class.
In fifth grade, I fell deeply in love with Taylor Hanson, the
androgynous middle brother in Hanson who played the
keyboard, sang like a girl, and, frankly, looked a lot like

me. When my bitter music teacher, Mr. Bell (real name), mocked them for being superficial pop stars, I argued, *Actually, they write all their own songs.*

I remember sitting at my desk in my bedroom with a piece of notebook paper and an envelope I'd addressed to an official Hanson fan club that I'd found online. I also had a map of the United States and a ruler. One inch meant a hundred miles, so I counted out ten inches from Phoenix to Tulsa—where Taylor lived—and I began the letter, *Dear Taylor, I'm only a thousand miles away from where you are.* It seemed like a manageable distance—the kind that could be traveled through sheer will. One day, we would meet, and he would know what I knew: that I was young, sure, but I was the only one who could really love him.

I never saw Hanson in concert, I never got a letter back, and loving Taylor became so deeply uncool that I gave up and found a replacement. By sixth grade, I was in love with one of the Backstreet Boys—Brian, the seemingly asexual, nonthreatening Christian who loved playing basketball. Alexis loved AJ, which was no surprise, since he was the clearly designated "bad boy" of the group. Our friend Casey loved Nick, the obvious heartthrob with blue eyes and a blond bowl cut.

My love for Brian was fierce, and it was perpetuated by Alexis and Casey, since the group was our main topic of conversation. We wrote entire notebooks full of stories in which we were in high school with the Backstreet Boys before they were famous. Chapter by chapter, they fell in love with us. Even if we'd known the term, we would never have dared to call what we wrote "fan fiction," because that would imply the stories weren't true—and though we knew we invented everything, it seemed true to us. Or it seemed true to me. Alexis and Casey loved admiring the Backstreet Boys, but I secretly thought of myself as the most devoted of us. What I wrote wasn't meant to be entertaining, it was meant to change fate's course.

I knew how famous they were, and that they were in their twenties while we were only thirteen, but it's hard to explain how *close* they felt. I filled an entire wall with magazine photos of the Backstreet Boys, and I looked at them with such focus and for such long periods of time that it became like a prayer. It was the first time in my life that I remember feeling physical side effects of longing—I preferred to ache than to feel nothing at all. Someday, I would reach out and touch Brian and he would touch me—but when?

My mother took Alexis, Casey, and me to see the Backstreet Boys in concert about a year after our obsession began. I wrote Brian's nickname, "B-ROK," on my forehead in metallic blue eyeliner, and Alexis wrote AJ's nickname, "BONE," on hers. Inside the stadium, it was mostly girls like us and our mothers, filling the stadium with our electricity. Casey said, *We're about to breathe the same air as them*, and we screamed.

We were seated at least two hundred feet away from the stage, but we yelled their names as if they could hear us. They sang all our favorite songs, but I spent the entire show distracted, waiting for Brian to look at me. And then, toward the end of the show, he waved in my direction, and I felt it. *He looked at me!* I screamed in Casey's ear. *Did you see that?*

A few hours later, around midnight, I was in bed listening to the radio, trying to fall asleep. I loved pop music, of course, but the radio station I had playing that night was the alternative rock station that played at least one Nirvana song every hour. It certainly wasn't the kind of station on which you'd expect to hear a Backstreet Boys song playing, but I felt I'd already had my fill that evening.

Suddenly, the DJ announced, *Ladies and gentlemen, we have Nick Carter in the studio this evening. Yes, that's Nick Carter from the Backstreet Boys.* I immediately sat up in my bed to listen: he was there promoting his friend's rock band. I didn't wait to hear the details; I picked up my lime-green phone and dialed the radio station's number.

Everyone in my house was asleep, so I kept the volume on my stereo low and I kept my ear next to the speaker as the phone rang. Someone at the radio station picked up and asked if I would please hold—I said yes and waited. Nick played his friend's band's song, which I don't remember, and then they started letting callers talk to Nick. Then came call after call of mocking disgust and hate and accusing him of being gay, until the DJ would have to cut the caller off. About five calls in, I heard the DJ and my phone say the same thing: *Hello, you're on the air with Nick Carter.*

My adrenaline was pumping hard. I didn't know how to say what I actually wanted to say, which was, *Will you tell Brian that I love him?* I was old enough to know that was impolite, so I settled on a breathless *I just wanna say . . . that I love you and Brian. I was at your concert tonight, and it was amazing.* The DJ and Nick laughed and thanked me, then asked me what I thought of the song they played. I could barely hear them over my own heartbeat, so I misheard them as asking what I thought of the concert, and I said, *I was dancing the whole time.* They laughed and thanked me again and hung up.

I lay in my dark room with the radio still playing, but I wasn't listening. Having just seen the Backstreet Boys play to a sea of girls, and mentally multiplying that by the number of cities I knew they'd toured in, Brian had started to feel farther away than usual. But now I'd brought him closer again. Nick would tell Brian that I loved him, and then he'd know.

The next day, I called to tell Casey what had happened, since Nick was her favorite. She didn't believe me, but I'd recorded the conversation onto a cassette tape for exactly this reason, so I played it to her over the phone. *Did you hear that?* I asked her. *Yes. Wow,* she said calmly. I hadn't expected her to be jealous, but I understood it then. I saved the tape for myself and played it over and over and over again.

◆

In the 1982 German horror film *Der Fan*, Simone is a high school girl who falls in love with a famous pop star, known to the world only as R. She writes love letters to him constantly and devotes her life to waiting for a response from him. We see her leaving the dinner table without eating, isolating herself, and running out of class, unable to focus on anything but R. *I'm in my room listening to your latest record,* she writes in one of her letters. *It's wonderful, lovelier than the loveliest dream. It's as if you wrote it especially for me. It's as if we've known each other all our lives and shared every moment.*

*I know you understand me better than anyone and I understand you. I know we've been together in our hearts from the beginning of time. Why is fate keeping us apart like this?*

Simone is beautiful like a model but ignores the affections of a male classmate—at one point, she tosses aside a cassette tape he gives her. She only wants R, and, in a letter, asks him to wink at her on a television show so that she'll know he received her letter. After getting in a fight with her parents, she is unable to watch the whole performance, so she writes another letter: *All you have to write is one word: "yes," and I'll come to you like a shot.*

When my high school photography teacher assigned a portrait project, I asked Adam, a nineteen-year-old I was infatuated with. *Sure, I'll be your model*, he said, the way he said everything: as if he looked forward to breaking my heart. He wasn't my boyfriend by any means, but he always said yes to me, and then he'd find a way to make it difficult—he'd complain, show up late, cancel at the last minute. One time he offered to take me to Lollapalooza and then just never showed up. No one had ever driven me insane in this way. I was in my room next to my lime-green phone, waiting for an explanation to light up my life. My hope kept me alive, as it did with so many things then. I was sure that Adam would arrive at any moment and we'd go, and I'd forgive him, and we'd have the best time. As the hours passed, I cried and raged with the heat of my realization, but I reacted privately. And because I wasn't witnessed, I couldn't be sure that I hadn't imagined myself. I'd have to see him again so he could know what I knew: that I'd rather die than be ignored.

Adam's house was in the middle of the desert, in Scottsdale, about forty-five minutes north of my parents' house. There were no streetlights where he lived—a surefire sign that everyone in the neighborhood was wealthy. The dirt road was bumpy and felt like work. One time, I encountered a wild white horse standing in the middle of the road, and we stared at each other for so long I thought I might have entered another world. And maybe I had: a world where my parents could only reach me by phone, a world where I was alone with a man who had his own house in the middle of nowhere. My driver's license and my curiosity were the only things I needed, so they were the only things I took. One night, Adam and I watched *Silence of the Lambs* lying on our sides. When the girls cried out from their pit, Adam asked, *What do I have to do to kiss you?* and I said, *You only have to turn me over.*

Adam claimed to own his own island, but when I asked to see photos of it, he said he'd never been there. I chose to believe the lie because the lie was beautiful. Once, I drove us to a Wendy's parking lot, and we dipped french fries into a chocolate Frosty as he talked about the island. If he invented enough details, he could believe in it, too.

I used to call Adam after he got drunk—the calls lasted longer that way. He'd usually complain about other women and then say something like, *That's why you're better.* What he meant was, *You're younger*—I hadn't had time to ruin anyone yet. I liked that he was older but had nothing of value to pass on, nothing to teach me. It was a relief to never receive advice.

I didn't love him but I was fascinated by him, which did

feel like love at first. He'd kiss me and say, *Like this*. He'd approach me at a party and say, *You*. A small amount of affection sustained me for weeks. I'd wonder how I'd accessed that one part of him and then I'd become desperate to access it again.

In my high school darkroom, I developed the photos I'd taken of Adam. I'd photographed different parts of his body, different angles of his face. It was a relief to finally be able to worship him in private. The laboriousness of developing the film felt good, as if I was doing a job. I'd been told all my life that I'd get what I wanted as long as I worked hard enough. So I worked on Adam—studying him, arranging his body in tubs of chemicals. I used tongs to submerge the paper deep enough to develop. At first, the paper was white. Then, suddenly, it was him.

◆

In *Der Fan*, Simone stands outside a television studio, waiting for R to arrive. She still hasn't received a response to her letters, but her hope keeps her alive. Then R drives up, and fans surround the car as he signs autographs. Simone stands twenty feet away, far from the crowd, just staring at him. He seems to feel her gaze on him and he looks up to meet it, then approaches her. Simone's eyes widen; she's in shock. *Don't you want an autograph?* R asks her. No response. *Tell me, what's your name, then?* No response. *Well, you had your chance.*

But as R walks away, Simone faints, and when she wakes up, she is lying down inside the television studio, and R is sitting beside her, holding her hand. She looks at his eyes and then their hands, as if to determine whether or not she's dreaming, and then back at his eyes, staying silent. She has reached him without uttering a word.

I was hired as a sales associate at a twenty-four-hour FedEx Kinko's, which meant I spent most of my after-school hours taking new print orders or ringing people up for their completed orders. The people I worked with were bizarre— one guy grew up in the circus; one girl was nocturnal; my boss didn't exercise because he believed humans were born with a predetermined number of heartbeats and he didn't want to waste his. Sometimes men would call and breathe heavily into the phone, getting off on my surprise, but mostly people wanted to know things like how to make a single black-and-white copy of their driver's license. It was an easy job, and I did it well.

There was a section of the store called the "office center" where you could plug your laptop in and work, but it was very rarely used. Then, a couple months after I started my job, I noticed a man who had begun working there every day for several hours. His workstation was about five feet to the left of my register and separated from it only by a glass partition. I don't know how long he had been watching me when I first noticed it—had I ignored days of this? I felt his gaze, I turned to meet it, and he looked away. It went on like this for weeks: I'd come in for my shift after school; he'd come in shortly after I arrived and leave shortly before I left. He was in his midthirties, with red, acne-scarred skin and a stiff walk. He didn't appear to be doing any work, and he wasn't making any copies, but there was no way to ask him to leave because he was technically allowed to sit there as long as he wanted. No one else seemed to give him any thought.

A few weeks later, I rode my bike to a Barnes & Noble near my school before going home. I sat down at a table with a magazine, but after about twenty minutes, I felt the urge to look up. There, half behind a bookshelf, I saw the man from my job watching me. When my eyes met his, he turned. I got up and walked toward him, not sure what I would say if he stopped, but he didn't stop—he walked straight out of the store. I followed him outside and stood near the entrance while he unlocked his car door. The only way for him to leave was to drive past me, so that's what he did, looking straight at me. I looked back at him, so he would know that I knew. I wrote down his license plate number because it seemed like the only thing I could do.

After that, I told my parents what had happened and what had been happening, and they called the police. An officer came over to file a report, and he sat in the rocking chair that my mother had used to breastfeed me and my sister when we were babies. The chair creaked with his weight; I could see his gun underneath the armrest. I had cried on my bike ride home from the bookstore, convinced I was doomed, that the man was probably watching me from his car at that very moment, finding out where I lived, plotting my intricate kidnapping or my murder, but with the cop there, I felt calm and stoic. I also felt like a celebrity being interviewed. *When did you first notice him? Does he always watch you when you're at work?*

I didn't have the right details for everything I'd seen—I could explain most of the where and the when, but not the *feeling* (that old female word) that something was wrong. I looked at the gun on the cop's hip again—it felt odd to see it so accessible, so ready. I thought of the word *order*, because it seemed as if the questions were part of a routine, and that the routine might keep me safe.

But there was nothing that he could do, not even with a license plate number. Without a direct threat, he explained that I'd have to *wait it out.* I asked, *Wait for what?* and he said, *For him to do something that gives you a reason to call 911.* He said I should keep going to work but that I shouldn't be alone in public anymore or ride my bike anywhere. He prescribed these things like medicine, like something easy to take.

My parents told my boss, and my boss asked that I come in to go over old security footage. That way, we could find an image of him and point him out to the other employees. We sat in his office with the tinted windows in the back of the store and went through tape after tape—I couldn't remember the last day I'd seen him. *There!* I said. *That's him*, but I hadn't realized my boss didn't have a tape in the VCR. *That's the live footage*, he said, and we turned, and we could see him, but he couldn't see us. My boss hurried to put a blank tape in the machine and pressed the red Record button so we could keep him.

I stayed in the office for about a half hour, until he lost interest and left. The other employees were briefed on the situation and, over the next few days, as I went back to work, they began watching him back. There was still no legitimate reason to kick him out. Every day he'd sit there and stay silent and watch me complete my dull tasks: pressing buttons, giving change.

Then, one day, he packed up and began to leave, but this time he paused halfway to the door and looked back at me—something he'd never done before. I stood still, focusing on him, waiting for something to happen. The fluorescent lights and the copiers hummed around us like a cicada song. My body had evolved to read his. I could tell he was never coming back, and he never did.

Simone, in R's bed: *But I thought you needed me?*

I felt calm, in control, older. Nothing could touch me, and nobody did. Later that night, I placed a man's driver's license facedown on a copy machine while a bright green laser scanned his face, then my arm, so that the printed copy documented both of us. *That's okay*, he said, *I only need this part*. I thought about my part, the movie I was writing in my head. Could I be the star? Admiration was part of that answer, instinct was another. I learned one new language each day.

Swollen and Victorious

Hands are unbearably beautiful.

They hold on to things. They let things go.

—MARY RUEFLE, "The Cart"

## 1. The Heart Line

*Wanna see my hand?* a woman asked me as I walked alone—
but it wasn't a question, just a way of showing it to me
there on the street in the middle of the night. Sure enough,
bloody, parts of it were dry but it was a new thing, like a
prize.

On that street in Brooklyn, it was wise to not talk to
anyone, not look anyone in the eye, be as invisible as possible, walk faster the later it was. The cold deterred some
people, but then you knew for sure the figures you did see
would have something to show you—a knife, a smile that
glowed in the dark, a hand that's been somewhere.

*It's really bad; see?* Another question that didn't mean
anything. She was walking with me now—her hand looked
redder under the deli's neon sign, but hell if I was going to
open a dialogue in twenty degrees. The weather had been
so unreliable that week, I kept dressing wrong—it was
T-shirt weather one day, parka the next. Funny how even
those of us who want to die care about dressing for the
day. This was one of those weeks I wanted to die, but not
from exposure—something more glamorous. Something
holy or ugly. I felt I could get this right.

So many people need no encouragement; they just stay with you, dead or not—like this woman presenting her awful hand. What am I supposed to do with that—invite her into my home and give her a Band-Aid? Sympathize? Tell her that the last time I was bleeding in the street, I asked for it?

I found the wildest guy I knew—we'd known each other in another town but we were both in Brooklyn now, both lonely now. I ate one meal per day now: a twelve-inch turkey sandwich with everything on it from the place with the neon sign under the J train. That's all I could afford, and it kept me full, but then I'd drink whiskey at night and become feral.

*Come on, hit me*, I said. *Don't be a pussy. Hit me in the face.* Even my weakness sounded strong sometimes. He laughed hard, knowing he was about to hit a girl, maybe for the first time ever, who would do that? I guess anyone who looked at me too long with my begging face shining like the moon would do that. I'd always wanted to know what it felt like—in Tucson I'd loved men who believed violence was the answer, and they hit each other until they got it right. One time I saw a man go down in the alley behind the diner and, later, I held the hand that hit him. It was so big I had to use both of my hands to cradle it—*swollen and victorious*, I'd said.

And then I'd convinced my friend to really punch me—a fist coming toward me, across my nose. I said *Ow* because I thought it would hurt, my voice came in before my body felt anything, *Ow*, isn't that what people said when they got hit? I saw stars, actual cartoon stars, and they were beautiful even then, not just now in my memory. How many things are beautiful in the moment you experience them? I fell to the ground and he was laughing above me, asking if I was okay, touching the blood from my nose.

I started laughing then, too, remembering we were in public with so many windows that could've been looking. *Joy*, I just remember thinking. When had I last felt that? Children feel joy, right? They must. They can't just whine about justice all day long—what's fair. Who gets what. Blah blah. I loved being an adult and being broke but living. I had so little, but all of it was mine: my leather jacket, my unlimited MetroCard, my shelf of books that seemed like clues.

I knew my friend would do whatever I asked of him, so I only asked for things I really wanted, like dinner with me at my apartment a few months prior. We split a can of potato soup diluted with milk, and then we made a salad with romaine lettuce, red onion, and croutons. He put olive oil, lemon juice, salt, and pepper on it; that was it. *Tastes like summer*, I said, and I closed my eyes and listened to the radiator clicking away behind us. It was great the way we never kissed and still got what we wanted, or at least I did. I never felt lonely as a child; social things were always someone else's idea. But try having your first real adult birthday alone with your ex-boyfriend who pities you and then you'll get it. I did.

*Can we go inside?* my sister asked, and it wasn't until then I realized she had been there the whole time—watched me get hit, fall back, laugh hard. She was on the steps, numb from witnessing how I acted when no one was looking. But she was looking, the windows were looking; I just forgot about the world sometimes. She'd come into town to sleep in my bed and *see a show* and here I was, giving her everything. The three of us went upstairs, behind closed doors, but my friend and I weren't done—we'd removed something from each other and then we couldn't put it back. He grabbed a butcher knife from the kitchen and chased after me—I laughed so hard I fell to the ground in the hallway. He pinned me down and put the knife to my throat while my sister closed the door to my room. *You can't do anything now, can you?* One of those questions that's more of a comment. I laughed because I couldn't believe how much he loved me. What a person. It's so rare you just look at someone and think: what a person. Our loneliness went out with our breath, but then we had no choice but to breathe it back in.

The knife stayed on my throat for I don't know how long. We needed a prop to act well, to manufacture a storm that swallowed us both, to bleed through my nose and remember, remember turning a year older and wanting to go backward or forward, anywhere but now, here, asking my friend, *Can we go somewhere?* He didn't answer because he didn't have to; the city went quiet and soft and no one bled and no one died and no one had a sister and no one had a friend and no one looked out of their window and no one ever witnessed anyone else.

God, we got away with everything then, didn't we?

## 2. The Life Line

But before all this, there was Tucson, where you had to put a towel over your steering wheel if you'd left it in the sun for too long. My friends were always taking a quick trip to Nogales and getting tequila for cheap and then getting robbed of their money or their switchblades and then getting stopped at the border if they looked Mexican or were Mexican and then getting back late and telling us all about it. They didn't look like cowboys, but they acted as if we lived in Wild West times, and maybe we did.

I always hear stories about how insignificant we are, how alone we are, how the universe is expanding and aren't we so small, isn't our English so adorable, so prone to disappearance. And yet, one person's hand can change a life—one palm, one touch. Like, how about the immeasurable electricity between two hands about to meet for the first time, how about the texture of a hand on my face versus my forearm versus my thigh, how about the heat of a slap meant as a placeholder for love or harm, you decide. I've had hands around my neck that turned from lust to violence. I knew I could die, but still I didn't fight. Survival of the fittest—a game some choose not to play. I thought if he felt so strongly, then maybe that's how it ends. That's how much I love the world—I accept my mortality, my temporality, my weakness, my choice to be held, to disappear.

Say it with me: *brutality.* Say it with me: *history.*

I could be a beacon of light, I could understand someone for once. My hand is the wave when it breaks. My hand is the city when it lights up at night. My hand is the knife when I karate-chop his thigh. Hi. Yah. You're. Mine.

In Tucson, in school, everyone was teaching me something, or I was listening to strangers talk and forming a lesson out of it. Everything seemed like a message just for me, that's how desperate I was. I was hungry to emerge from my life victorious, or at least to do something that looked like winning. Blood seemed like a trophy, no matter who it belonged to.

One of my journalism class requirements was to attend a court trial. At the front entrance, my class had to wait for me, because the carabiner I used as a keychain was deemed dangerous. *How is that a weapon?* I asked the security guard, and he put his four fingers through it and said, *Brass knuckles, like this.* I left it for him to discard and took my keys to the hall, where my class was waiting.

The courtroom was dark and cold, just the way I thought it would be. But it was sleepier than I'd imagined, like a theater: lighted up front, and we could barely see our notebooks in back. Our class filled most of the otherwise empty room, and the Border Patrol officer on trial looked at us as he walked in, trying to figure out why we were there. I accidentally made eye contact, which seemed so confrontational I gasped. I felt as if I was watching TV, but then suddenly the TV was watching me. This was my first courtroom— I didn't realize how private it felt, as if we'd walked in on his secret. And indeed, whatever happened that night on the Arizona-Mexico border was between him and the family of the man he shot and killed.

Inside the courtroom, we all tried to unravel that secret, we tried to find the truth. The family was Mexican, trying to cross the desert undetected, and they were unlucky enough to encounter a white man with a gun. The angle of the bullet showed the victim had been on his knees, in a surrender position, but he was killed anyway—*self-defense.* I realized then that I'd be a bad journalist because all I wanted to do was write about the Border Patrol officer's face—how it moved and contorted as the evidence was revealed, as the prosecution brought out a poster board with a diagram that illustrated the journey of the bullet. In my mind, he was guilty. A good journalist fights for justice, checks people in power, sees both sides. *Unbiased*—what a word.

I was as biased as they come. I thought it was because I was a woman, because seventy-five percent of each month was consumed by blood—one week of being about to bleed, one week of bleeding, one week of having just bled. Exhibit A: me crying because something was *too beautiful*. How could I be trusted to tell someone's story when all I could do was imagine the dark of the desert, my own fear of encountering this man alone in the middle of the night?

The man with the gun saw the man on his knees and pulled the trigger that changed everyone's lives, even mine. It was the first time I saw a man try to justify a killing, how he told a story to himself and then performed that story for us. *Testimony*—a lovely word made ugly right there, right then. I never made eye contact with him again, I just wrote notes in my notebook, I learned how to write different words than the ones I was listening to. With my class with me there—even then, I felt alone. I thought about how alone we all are. In the same room, in the same country. A wall is built, someone walks around it. A border closes, a hand reaches through.

### 3. The Head Line

I stayed on my journalism path, assumed changing majors was too much of a hassle, thought maybe someday I'd find a way to put myself into the story. I did my homework and I drank whiskey and I touched women's faces when I kissed them. I couldn't figure out where women belonged— behind a microphone or in front of a camera? Women had this way of being invisible unless tragedy was assigned to them.

I don't remember what Gabrielle Giffords and I talked about the night we met in 2008, but I remember how we smiled in the photo afterward. I don't remember what her speech was about, but I remember she made a joke about the audience hoping to hear from her husband, real-life astronaut Mark Kelly, but being "stuck" with her, a Tucson congresswoman, instead. I don't remember which of the other undergrad students wanted to be an astronaut, I don't remember what the requirements were besides learning to scuba dive and speaking Russian, and I don't remember wanting anything at that time in my life besides enough love and enough money to live on.

I don't remember how I found out that Gabrielle Giffords had been shot, but I was in Los Angeles by then, three years after we'd met, watching the news on my laptop while teens smoked pot in the alley by my bedroom window. I don't remember all the details, so I've looked some up: Jared Lee Loughner, twenty-two at the time, went to a "Congress on Your Corner" event that Giffords was hosting outside a Safeway supermarket in Tucson. Loughner used a 9-millimeter Glock pistol to shoot Giffords in the head, then killed six other people and injured thirteen. The morning of the shooting, Loughner posted a photo on his Myspace page that showed his gun sitting on what appeared to be a textbook—the title read, *United States History*.

I remember sitting there in a kind of dazed horror, the way I had when I first learned about the Columbine shootings. I don't remember crying when I learned about Columbine—it felt far away somehow, as if it had happened on another planet. I remember some kids stayed home from school the day after, but that didn't make sense to me—how could violence like that reach us, there, then? It hadn't, and so it couldn't.

But I knew that Safeway, I knew that local news station, I knew that reporter, I knew that Loughner was only a year older than me, I knew that Giffords wasn't fake like other politicians—I knew that because I'd touched her hand once, and I believed what she said that night, if only I could remember it.

Girls like me—we get to choose when and where to look. We get to choose for how long and when to turn away—that's the real privilege. I think I can train myself to look longer, to remember more, to write more down when I can't remember, to give testimony worth recording, to learn from it. I think a hand might be the same thing as language, I think it might be more efficient. I think blood might be the first story of touch, I think it might have a hundred endings, I think I want to live long enough to see them all.

*Artist Statement*

I think I wrote it, in a way, to try to find you.

—JESSE TO CELINE in *Before Sunset*

I'm trying to think of the hole in my bathroom ceiling as something besides a metaphor, but I can't—when I feel hopeless, I turn things into other things. How could the hole not be a wound, bleeding with clues to the past? How could the hole not be a woman, leaking a little every time my upstairs neighbor takes a shower? I know, it's an old building, it's a bad pipe, it's a slumlord's fault. I know, and yet.

I'm trying to write my life down before it's too late. I don't know why I become more afraid the more I write. I don't know why I can't override that feeling of being afraid of what will come out: who I'll hurt next, who I'll betray, what world I'll trespass into this time. When I told my friend I was out of ideas, he said, *Write about not having any ideas.*

I'm trying to remember all the times art saved me. Art can be so good that it consumes me. Being consumed is an act of salvation—I give myself up to the possibility of true light. Whenever I encounter genius in another person's work, I give myself over to it, hoping to forget myself, hoping to touch it for real for at least a moment. All the better if the writer or artist is still alive—that means geniuses aren't finished being born yet.

I'm trying to write about someone without giving away his identity. I could say, *Well, he's got this face that's alive like the tide and lit like the moonlight, no matter what time it is.* I could say, *Well, he's got this special power where he gazes in a way that makes time stop.* He says, *Will you write my biography someday?* and I say, *I'll write your autobiography today.* That's not giving him away—he's beyond dialogue, beyond description. That doesn't mean I'm done attempting.

I'm trying to enforce the household rule: no discussion of nuclear war after midnight. That's always when it comes up, when the headlines of the day have sunk in, when I open up to the possibility that language could die soon, and then where would our work go?

I'm trying to check the locks less. When I leave my apartment, I become convinced I've left the door unlocked and that someone will rob me of all my possessions—I'll come home to a door ajar and nothing left. I've never been robbed, but I obsess over this image. I lock the door, I hear it click, I walk a few paces, then I have to go back. Sometimes when I leave the door, I say out loud to myself, *The door is locked, the door is locked.*

I'm trying to describe how it feels to know you, but I just keep coming back to this memory of camping when I was very young, around eight years old. Someone told me there were beavers that emerged in the early morning to make their dams in the river. I awoke the next morning at dawn, the way children are known to do in anticipation of a great event. I looked to my father, who was sound asleep, and then put my shoes on, unzipped the tent, and began walking. I walked for a long way, excited at the prospect of seeing something brand new. On my walk, I lost my way and became so disoriented that I couldn't remember my name when a stranger saw me and asked. He said, *Let's get you back*, and part of me didn't want to go. I didn't know where I was going, but I hated to think I was heading back to where I started. I never saw the animals in their act, I never saw how they make a wall in the river, I never found out how they do it. But for some reason, I got lost trying to catch a glimpse of it. That's the best way I can describe you to someone.

I'm trying to think of the word *wall* without thinking about Mexico, but the news just takes over my mind like that sometimes, even if I try to shut it out, even if I look away. The images and voices creep back in, at the airport or the gym, reminding me of the state of the world, the things someone said on repeat, *Wall wall wall, we're going to build a wall to keep the bad people out.*

I'm trying to stop using love as an antidote to end times. Part of me thinks it won't matter what I do because the world will end before our love does. When everything seems on the verge of collapse, I don't know what to do besides indulge every desire. Help?

I'm trying to have faith in any form. When I was ten, my parents dropped my sister and me off at our grandmother's house. She took us to her church's Bible camp every day, where my sister and I were mocked by the other students for not knowing even the most basic facts about the Bible. Our parents never taught us, and we seemed to get along fine without it. But at Bible camp, the pastor and his wife were ventriloquists. I learned about God from a puppet's mouth, which made sense at the time. I believed I could ascend to a land of peace and forgiveness. I didn't have anything to be forgiven for yet, but I believed in the possibility of turning into an unimaginable adult. Look, here she is now, no longer believing in ascent.

I'm trying to find out why I fall into a trance sometimes and why I resent waking up from it. The world goes quiet when I am being bad again—I could live forever in that kind of silence. But then: confession, consequence, aftermath. It's enough to make a girl go good.

I'm trying to recall the man on my street who owned his own hot air balloon business. He took tourists up over the Phoenix desert in rainbow-colored balloons lifted by fire. On one particular trip into the sky, he crashed into some power lines, and a bag of cocaine fell out of his pocket. When I first heard about it, I imagined the cocaine falling straight into a police officer's hand. That's not how it happened, but I could see it so clearly in my mind, saw his balloon mangled and deflated on the news later, saw a new family move into his house when he went to jail, and never saw him again.

I'm trying to envision Earth as a woman: all I see are large hips made from tree roots, bowing outward, making way for all of us, none of us asking for life in the beginning but soon demanding more than she can give us. I hate writing *us*, but that's where I am: desperate times call for desperate ways to speak for everyone.

I'm trying to find a place with less noise. Last week, when I thought I'd escaped the sirens and shouting of New York in my yoga class, the fire alarm went off, so loud we had to cover our ears in warrior pose. Even then, no one left— we were used to that kind of auditory attack. We evolve and contort and accept.

I'm trying to speak to you in my dreams. Can you hear me calling out to you, animal to animal? What I emit are not words, not really, but they take a purposeful shape when uttered alone in the dark. The first language must have been invented out of desperation, out of pure instinct and need. That's how I sound.

I'm trying to say what I mean, without any stylistic interruptions. I don't regret what I've done, because if I didn't do it then, I would have done it later. I believe certain mistakes are imprinted into our DNA: it's only a matter of time before we make them.

I'm trying to write something so good, so pure, so perfect that I'll never have to have children; I'll have created something that can stand in for me, that can live on after me.

I'm trying to whisper something that can't be spoken aloud: *I still think about you.*

I'm trying to identify what drew me to the people I've loved. I seem to thrive in a state of in-between, of wanting to love all the way but only receiving a portion of what I want. That sliver is enough to make me want all of it—I feel the moon changing shape, and she feels me turning.

I'm trying to evolve into all wolf all the time. It seems possible if I let go of the idea of my body, if I fall into my dream headfirst, if I accept words as signals more than language, if my love sounds like a howl in the forest—doesn't it already?

I'm trying to promise you I won't leave again, but I can't guarantee it. You know how I am—can't decide on groceries, too distracted by the perfect white bars of soap in one aisle. Last summer, I stood there transfixed by their milky perfection; I said it looked like art or something. You left to shop without me—easier to leave me standing there in my admiration until I was done.

I'm trying to forget you; you must think I have by now. *Honor*— you always hated when I used that word—I'm trying to *honor* all the ways we knew each other, all the things we said, all the ways I saw your face change before our time was up.

I'm trying to document all the ways I angled toward the light and all the ways I leaned into shadows, every time I faced myself and every time I refused to look.

I'm trying to forget when and where I live, trying to leave my responsibilities behind. Call to me again, my love. Wave me down like a taxi cab in the middle of a summer so hot only the beautiful people lose their minds. I took my glove off so slowly you thought you'd die waiting. And what better way to end? You died as I lived: waiting to reveal myself.

I'm trying to use my small powers for good. What if I wasn't a villain? What if I was the hero of my life? What if I knew what a lesson was and learned it? In this moment, the horizon is calm but red with the dirt of my past. It's so easy to fill up my life with a person so wild I can't look away. I love the shapes we made together, I love the way we spoke in fragments, Sappho style; we took our time, we carved ourselves into stone. We were so desperate to unveil ourselves that we came out like poetry—secrets often do. But that was then, this is aftermath.

I'm trying to solve the math of my life, so complex it begins to surpass my abilities—$X$ equals me plus my capacity to imagine minus the way I make people fall in love divided by my true nature, my wildness like the lion that bit the actor's hand. That's the kind of viciousness that keeps me alive. How's that for a remainder? I am survival of the fittest, I am what endures when the Earth ends, I am exoskeleton instinct, alive with my own evolution.

I'm trying to outline all my contradictions. I am alive but not living. My heart beats but forgets. My legs walk but in the wrong direction. My phone lights up but does not ring. My ring stays on my finger but does not represent eternity. My face feels clean but becomes dirty. My mind wanders but does not leave. My computer hurts me but does not kill me. The bones in my feet break but heal. I am cold but not heartless. I wear headphones but only hear my own voice. I have a phone but only call one person. I wear black but feel blue. I want to see my friends but don't want to tell them about my life. I want to fall in love but I don't know how to be good. I want to be good but I think I was born bad. I did an ugly thing but it was in a beautiful room. I was pretending to be someone but you were believing it. My hair is dark but the source of your hope. I sent you a poem but you didn't listen to it.

I'm trying not to leave amidst hardship. I witness myself. I hear the rhythm of my body even if no one else hears it—I believe in it, and that's enough. I alternate between deciding I deserve the world and deciding I deserve nothing. There is no moderation in this day and age: it's life or death, it's mask or reveal, it's absolute truth or all lies. I pinned myself to the wall until I became desperation in its purest form. I must speak first, so that you know why I'm here, why I speak at all. If I don't get what I want, I'll die. If I get what I want, I'll die. Either way, I lived.

# Halfway Out the Door

I return to memories of the people who taught me something, even accidentally. I love them, not for who they are but for the ways in which they altered me. In this way, my love for them becomes a love for my own deterioration.

◆

The only thing worse than hearing your voice at its most desperate is recognizing it.

◆

Whenever I remember that dogs began as wolves, my hope for my own domestication returns.

◆

By the time I reached the living room, the front door was already open, and he was standing there with his keys in one hand, his phone in the other. I knew my mascara had stained my cheeks, but it was clear I didn't have time to wash it off—he wanted to take me home now. I zipped my dress up slowly; I couldn't quite get the metal through the holes on my shoes' ankle straps, I was taking forever. It's not that I thought we'd love each other, but I was so sad to have my answer in the doorway, to know for sure. I'd lived so long with the uncertainty that I began to mourn it like a little death, and I'm still mourning it, now, here, a thousand miles away.

◆

My friend, after running into his ex-girlfriend on the street: *It was really good. I felt really bad.*

♦

I'm unrecognizable behind the stories I tell, but I include just enough detail so everyone can see what I see: a hypothetical storage space in the hypothetical town where all my real lives go.

♦

No one acted afraid of me. That's how I knew I should become fearless.

♦

Everything I do is an effort to answer a question, even if the question is, *How selfish can I be?*

♦

In third grade, I had a friend who once let me sleep on her top bunk. That night, we watched television until her father came in and used his crutch to press the Off button. He was usually in Hawaii, studying geology, but this week he'd returned from the hospital with steel reinforcements protruding from his shin, keeping it intact. Earlier that night, he let us trace the metal with our fingers and he said, *I went to look at the volcano, but then it came to look at me,* and we laughed, and we imagined the world.

♦

I thought I wanted love all to myself, but as soon as I had it, I wanted everyone to know what I'd found, to know that I'd given it a new name.

◆

I can be convinced of any version of justice, if the wronged speak eloquently enough for long enough.

◆

My friend's mother had a car with a makeshift backseat that faced the wrong way, and we spent our rides home waving at the people driving behind us. They could either wave back or pass us, but both actions were forms of confrontation, and this was not beyond our young minds. We made people choose. That was our one power.

◆

It's almost kinder to keep the secret, I say to the secret person. He agrees. Almost.

◆

He slept with his back to me, which made me jealous of his dreams. *Hey. Hey. Wake up.*

◆

On a school trip to Washington, DC, my friend and I were allowed an unchaperoned hotel room. We went to sleep on time, too afraid of Room 118, where the boys from North Dakota told us to go. On the bus, they said their favorite thing to do was cow tipping. *We steal my dad's beer and go up to the barn and you pretty much just have to breathe on them.* That night I walked to the bathroom in my sleep and brought an empty plastic cup to my sleeping friend. The next morning, she told me, *You just kept saying it wasn't the right water. But then I kept bringing you water and you kept drinking it.*

◆

Being wrong feels better than being right because that means there's still somewhere left to go.

◆

A man I loved once referred to my disbelief regarding romance as a *running theme.*

◆

We kissed with the lights on, drank whiskey out of old bottles of ginger ale, went to sleep listening to the sounds of his roommates playing video games in the living room. I tried to remember what I'd liked about him at first. *His last name translates to* moon, I remembered. *His last name means the moon.*

◆

I waste so much time that I'm grateful when the world does it for me. Once a year, I get to write my favorite sentence: *We lost an hour in the night.*

◆

I've never witnessed either of my parents in an act of self-sabotage, but I must have learned it from somewhere.

◆

On the Internet, everyone's getting an award, everyone's buying new shoes, everyone's swimming at the beach, everyone's eating a wonderful meal. Here we are. Everyone's in love.

◆

*These are hands that have never played an instrument*, the man said in bed, holding my fingers with his. *I play guitar, actually*, I said, and he said, *No, you don't.*

◆

Each time the day ends, darkness appears as a mystery to my artist friend—wasn't today the day she would finally be recognized? She sees the world as *behind* her somehow, about to catch up. Soon she won't have to make anything.

◆

I could tell my boyfriend's new songs were about his exgirlfriend—the one who looked like me, the one with the same middle name as me, the one who left. I accepted my position as her replacement, sometimes I even reveled in it. I knew who those songs were about and I liked hearing him sing them.

◆

*I have nothing but fondness and affection for you*, I said, halfway out the door.

◆

Like any tool, heartbreak dulls.

◆

My best friend started doing meth, lost weight, bounced her leg all through algebra class. I watched her move as if her body was math, and it was—reducing each day. I felt like her remainder, left over from childhood. I spoke to her, but she couldn't hear me. I was on our old frequency.

◆

Being underestimated is a form of power.

◆

The high school badminton team was one way to wait for softball season to start, so we spent our afternoons with a coach who despised us. Toward the end of the season, we began regarding his rage with a kind of admiration—how fierce it was! We'd never felt so hated in all our lives. Whenever we lost, he'd speak with his back to us, as if we were so insignificant we didn't even deserve his voice. Whenever we won, he said, *That's more like it.*

◆

I long to be hung out to dry, to wave in the wind, to be made good. If religion was like that, I'd sit my flag body in the pews every Sunday. I'd confess, I'd make up for lost time, lost faith, lost wind, lost keys to the new world. Born bad but grew up to be a flag, marking all good ships.

◆

When I watched him cry so hard he could barely drive, I had just one thought: *This is the pain to make up for the pleasure, this is the pain to make up for the pleasure, this is the pain to make up for the pleasure.*

◆

When the astronaut spent a year in space, he grew two inches taller, just because he could.

◆

Specificity is a commodity and I'm saving up, up, up.

◆

His brutality reminded me of my own, but his was superior—I ached to keep up. In my spare time, I compiled harsh insults to unleash next time, but then he'd do something like punch a hole in the wall. We were bound by cruelty, which was sharper than love. He taught me that.

◆

I wrote so many poems about what might happen that I wasn't surprised when one of them came true. I tamed my outcomes, I built them—a train on its tracks.

◆

Suppose I fell in love with someone else, thought I could handle it, that I could manage it like an employee, as if my love worked for me. Suppose he said, *You're the one,* and I didn't say it back, couldn't, because I thought of other ones. Suppose love was a kind of focusing and refocusing. Suppose I could see.

◆

Greek chorus, come with me. Balcony set, stay here. I am the role of a lifetime and I let myself be played poorly. I believe in the potential of my terrible actor. I love my life; I also want it dead. That's the only honest thing I ever said.

◆

*I'm not explaining it right*, I said. *I'm leaving out the best parts.* I'd just begun, but then it was time to leave.

# Second Row

Joey was the tallest person I'd ever seen, even without the added height of the stage where I first saw him. I was seventeen; he was college-aged, but not *in* college, he was the singer of a band I never got tired of. He played guitar, too, but that was secondary to his voice, which was a kind of summoning.

The first time I entered Modified, the punk venue in the middle of the worst part of downtown Phoenix, I felt as if I'd finally found one good place. Everything was a strip mall or about to be a strip mall, and worse, there was some law about exterior paint resembling the mountains, so every building was painted beige. Phoenix looked terrible; the heat was terrible; my parents were terribly worried about me going downtown by myself every week, but they let me go anyway, and that's where Joey sang one night.

He did this thing with his legs—a spastic motion that didn't align with the drums, that seemed to come from another song inside of him. He closed his eyes when he sang, and I was glad for that, because then I didn't have to worry about him seeing the way I looked at him. It was embarrassing the way I kept going to Modified, paying five bucks at the door and milling around, waiting for someone to talk to me. Eventually, Anna did. She was like an older, cooler version of me, and we looked so alike that people asked if we were sisters. She liked that I was a few years younger than her—she wanted to be idolized, and I perpetuated that, made it real for her. It felt as if the entire city was asleep except for the fifty or so people inside Modified, and it was up to us to make something beautiful inside the ugliest city in the world. I didn't dare talk to Joey, but one night, he talked to me.

*Come to this party on Fifth and Hardy,* he said, holding my hand. *You can remember that 'cause it rhymes. The house with a big saguaro in front.* He was drunk, and I think he must have invited everyone and held everyone's hands, but I felt as if this was it—tonight our lives would merge. He got in the passenger side of his friend's car and waved goodbye to me, or maybe the guy next to me, and I jumped in my dad's car, a boxy 1987 Isuzu Trooper my friends called the Safari Mobile. I put the key into the ignition, and the stereo clock lit up: 11:15. The party was twenty minutes away, and my curfew was midnight, so I floored it down the I-10, thinking any punishment my parents imposed later would be worth it.

When I got there, I didn't see anything except dark houses—the worlds I'd correctly assumed were sleeping while everyone at Modified stayed up, falling in love. *Where is it?* I muttered to myself, determined to find that stupid cactus in the yard. I drove down every related side street, thinking maybe I was just early; the house must be right around here. But I drove and drove for a half hour, until I gave up and went home, and my parents didn't wake up when I unlocked the door ten minutes late, and that was the night Joey fell in love with Anna.

I nearly died the next week at Modified when I saw him leaning down to say something in her ear. *Happy birthday!* I said to Anna between bands. *Aw, thanks, pal!* she said, then asked, *You know Joey, right?* We smiled at each other, and I said, *I don't think we've ever officially met*, and then we touched hands for the second time. Joey left to go set up for his band's set, and I started questioning Anna. She was a little drunk, so she was happy to talk and didn't think it was weird that I asked questions like *Where does he live?* and *What do you guys do together?* She said Joey had a one-bedroom apartment by the railroad tracks, and the train went by once an hour, and the walls shook whenever that happened. She said Joey played folk records for her, and they were the best things she'd ever heard. The next week, I bought those records, and they were the best things I'd ever heard, too. I closed my eyes and thought of them on his mattress on the floor and of the twenty-four trains counting the hours. I thought of my conversations with Anna like research—perhaps one day my life would truly begin, and I'd be ready.

When summer started, Anna cut her hair, I cut mine, and Joey introduced us to his friend. Tyler looked a little like Joey, or maybe they just had similar noses. Tyler was studying creative writing in Seattle, but he was home for summer break. We started dating almost immediately. We stood next to each other at Modified shows, and held hands, and kissed when it was time for me to go home. We took Polaroids together, and I put them on the Internet to make them realer. One night, my parents were out of town, and Tyler rubbed his jeans against my jeans like someone lighting a hundred matches in a row. I closed my eyes and came, and then I asked Tyler if he wanted to go ahead and take my virginity. He said, *I'd just feel too bad*, and I didn't ask again. We went into the backyard so he could smoke another cigarette. He took the turquoise pack from his jeans pocket—American Spirits. *Isn't that what Joey smokes?* I asked, and he nodded as he lit the cigarette. One day, at Tyler's parents' house in Paradise Valley, he played me some folk records, but it was too late—I'd already heard them.

Joey had a friend whose parents owned an Asian-fusion restaurant chain and a mansion, so we all went there one night. It was full of people we didn't know—blond girls wearing heels and eating chips in the kitchen, guys wearing baseball caps and playing beer pong in the backyard. Anna and Joey had somehow known to wear their swimsuits, and they got in the hot tub. Tyler and I walked around the house, counting the bathrooms (nine), and then encountered a glass door that led to a stairwell to the basement. *Don't!* I said, as Tyler reached for the door handle. But he opened it, and a blast of cold air washed over us. We walked down the stairs and into the wine cellar. There must have been five hundred bottles in neat rows, kept at the perfect temperature. *Do you want some?* Tyler asked me, holding one he'd picked at random. *I don't drink*, I said, and he said, *Oh, right.*

Anna came over to Tyler's parents' house one day, and we all lay on the bed, spooning each other, falling asleep in the middle of the day. Where was Joey? He felt so far away, and yet we had touched him once. I want to say Joey ruined us, but that's not right—he taught us the meaning of longing, which means we didn't know the difference between loving him and wanting to love him, not yet. In 110-degree heat, it was hard to tell what was what. But if we couldn't be the songs he sang, at least we could be in the front row, or the second.

One night, Tyler and I sat on my driveway, talking about what would happen when he went back to college. He said he wanted to write a great novel by the time he graduated. When I asked him what he'd written so far, he said he was still in the *absorbing phase* of his life, and I thought, *Maybe I am, too.*

*Leaving Me*

I knew a girl in high school who shared my first name—she lured boys into her bedroom by saying, *I want to show you something*. She'd be in the passenger seat of some boy's car, they'd be in her driveway, and she'd say her line, just to see how quickly he'd pull the keys out of the ignition. She was beautiful enough that the boys would have gone into her room even if she didn't have a line, or if her line was a murder threat, but there each of my friends went, one by one, disappearing into the other Chelsea.

One of my friends lived to tell about her possessions: *Nothing to write home about*, he called the shelf of records and crystals and Polaroids, but I doubted it. Nothing's ever that simple—he was in love with her and couldn't tell her or something. I'm writing about the shelf now and I've never even seen it—that's what kind of girl she was.

Sharing a name with someone amplifies the element of competition: is the world big enough for two? I went wild with jealousy if I thought about her too much—her perfectly straightened hair, her tan, her ability to talk to boys with the confidence that she would one day *have* them. Her mother went to jail for a night because Chelsea illegally downloaded a thousand rap songs on her mother's computer and got caught, but it didn't matter. Even then, I longed to have her life, though I knew that was impossible. I wanted the unknown, the other, the superior version of myself, and I still do. I long and long—that word almost makes me love English again, makes me think I might be able to say what I mean.

Years later, in Los Angeles, I dreamt of a burning car the night before I saw it for real. The orange and blue flames danced in the middle of a downtown parking lot while I was three stories up in a neighboring building, remembering my dream. But even when it was real, it was fake—a movie set with men hosing it off.

*Lady with a Spear* is Eugenie Clark's 1953 memoir about her years as a fish scientist in Micronesia. She begins her book with a memory from age nine: *I took several fast deep breaths, adjusted my face mask, checked the safety lock on my speargun, and dived back down into the Red Sea.* Clark writes, *That may read like science fiction, or a dream. It isn't fiction, but it is a dream.*

With their boat anchored near a kelp bed, a navy instructor briefed Clark and a group of men on the signals used underwater for speaking to the ship: *One tug on the signal cord by the diver tells the tender, "I'm all right." Two tugs meant "Give me more line, I'm going farther away," three tugs meant "Take up slack, I'm coming in closer," and four tugs meant, "Danger, pull me up fast."*

When Clark went fishing with her spear, she wrote, *It's one thing to look down at the reefs through a glass-bottomed box or boat—another to be under the sea yourself, swimming freely among the reefs and seeing clearly in every direction.* I like Clark's descriptions of spear fishing and of the satisfaction of seeing something and making it hers.

*Are you going undercover?* the librarian asked me once as I checked out books about private investigators. I said, *If I were, do you think I'd tell you?*

In Brooklyn, I live with my partner, Mark, who says the most wonderful things sometimes. Last week, he said, *Sometimes it feels like we're in the future. I can't explain it; it's just this feeling that we're not in the right time.* I knew what he meant by that. Some days felt very long, some days felt impossibly short. I felt as if time couldn't exist the way clocks insisted it did. There was no way I could possibly be wasting this much of my life.

Last year, Mark went to Germany for three weeks to show his drawings at a gallery. I was left alone in our apartment and, after two weeks, I began hearing a bird in the backyard. I texted Mark, *It's like a bird from the jungle, unlike anything I've ever heard.* I didn't hear it all the time, but when I did, it was all I could hear. I had to leave the room or put headphones on. It sang the same notes each time, like a ringtone—piercing and exact. I put my phone near the window to try to record it to send to Mark in Germany, but when I played the recording back, I couldn't hear the bird at all.

One night I woke up at three in the morning to the sound of the bird. I groaned, got up to get my headphones from the other room, turned on my white noise app, and went back to sleep. When I awoke hours later, the bird was still chirping wildly. I wondered if it'd be there forever. Mark and I always joked that as soon as we got rid of one sound nuisance, another emerged. When the upstairs neighbor quieted her barking dog, another neighbor paced outside our window, talking on the phone. One sound replaced another. Hearing the shrill backyard noise, I texted Mark, *The mystery bird is the new enemy of silence.*

When Mark returned, I said, *If you hear the bird, you'll know it right away; it's the worst. And yet it's been silent since you've been back.* As soon as he asked, *Are you sure you didn't imagine it?* I realized I might have.

Most people with auditory hallucinations hear voices, like Joan of Arc and the saints in her head, but I've found some cases of hearing music without any auditory stimulus. Mental disorders like schizophrenia can cause auditory hallucinations, but so can stress, starvation, depression, and lack of sleep. Many people hear voices or music right before they go to sleep or when they wake up from a dream.

I knew a schizophrenic girl in high school who hallucinated forest scenes wherever she went—deer, trees, garden gnomes. *There's one,* she'd say to her boyfriend, and he'd turn to look. That's how we knew he loved her.

So what if there's no explanation for what I heard? What if there's no way to know for sure, no trauma to the brain? I could be unexplained, which means anything is possible, which means I see the water and think it's the sky.

Clark wrote that the earliest fish had three eyes, and their fossils show a small opening in the center of the skull. This held the *pineal eye*—the one that looked for light.

It seems I might be able to pretend anything into existence. I can paint a portrait in my mind and I never have to show it to anyone. It might be my greatest work: inventing the problems of my life.

Uncertainty, I address you because *you* are the problem, like when I was unqualified to teach middle school but I taught it anyway. One boy was so bad that I lost any authority I might have faked early on—the class became nothing more than a scheduled time each day devoted to paying attention to him. I wrote math equations on the whiteboard, but no one learned anything besides what my voice sounded like when I said *you*. I wondered if this was how great men were made. I wondered if I was making one.

No one was in the burning car, no one was in danger. It was roped off; it was Los Angeles at night, of course it was a movie. Now the image serves as an anchor—I can't help but return. How many truths have I blazed through, not listening? Take up slack, I'm coming in closer. I will find my way back to the beginning, back to you.

I once knew a man with a reputation so bad that I decided I needed to see him up close, examine him like a bottle of something that makes you forget. I don't know what I thought I'd find—nothing is hidden. Everyone is so obvious, and we flatter ourselves by thinking otherwise. But lust defies all logic, and thank god for that. No one ever fell in love with a math equation. Or if they did, they married it and lived in a place I never saw, a place where people live happily ever after, and that's not New York.

In New York, I met the man with the reputation at the bar with the televisions. Talking about the art museum, he said *trident*, held up three fingers, asked, *Is that what I mean?* I thought he meant *triptych*, but I didn't know for sure. We barely knew each other that night, but it was an intimate question because he asked me to enter his mind, to find his meaning for him, so I did.

I moved my hand from the edge of the bar to my glass so slowly that I thought he might say something, but he didn't notice. When I washed my hands in the bar bathroom later, it was religious how long I took to lather my hands and re-apply my lipstick. With every movement my body made, I grew further from myself until I was all pretend, I was *other*. I slowed down the process so I wouldn't miss it. But then he kissed me, and it felt like the start of a race. *Go.*

We walked in the cold back to his apartment, and I liked the way our shadows appeared and disappeared under the streetlights. I liked who I was with him, I knew it right away, and I became very focused. If it weren't for the red numbers on his clock, time wouldn't have passed or I wouldn't have thought about it. Anything seemed plausible, that's what uncertainty did. My heart was a dictator, and I invaded lands on its behalf. His room: mine. His bed: mine. His toothpaste I squeezed onto my index finger and rubbed against my gums: also mine. In bed, I held his arm up by the wrist and named his hand after me. I'd found him.

Lust resists meditation and encourages impulse. Lust absorbs everything, especially insight. My lust conceals the faces of strangers: Is he there? Or there? Everyone could be him.

(Did I keep you alive by looking at you? I'd like to think that.)

Strangers are the only perfect people—that's why I keep collecting them, that's why I see myself as a stranger and I love her better. I barely know her.

I wore salmon-colored cotton underwear the first time a boy touched me. His dog's name was Chelsea, and he told her to leave the room.

The Starbucks cashier in Midtown motioned for me to step down to his register. *He must be seven feet tall*, I thought as I handed my credit card to him. He looked at it, said *Chelsea*. That was the first time I'd heard my name spoken out loud in days, and he seemed to notice the stirring this provoked in me. *Chelsea, Chelsea, getting her coffee*, he said, returning my credit card to my open palm, *Chelsea, Chelsea, leaving me.*

Everything has its opposite, a mirror version of what it could be, if only: moon and satellite, island and houseboat, monument and illusion.

I remember the view from my friend Sarah's trampoline in her backyard. When we bounced high enough, we could see her neighbor, asleep in a lounge chair beside his pool. He was fit and tan, and his stomach muscles glistened like a cartoon. With every leap, we caught a glimpse of him and stored him away for later.

But what about the boy from our class who lived four doors down from the trampoline? What about the garage where he used his father's gun to shoot himself in the tenth grade? What about the girls who mocked him relentlessly when he was alive and cried for themselves when he wasn't? What about the way the swim team lit candles in the pool in his memory? What about the time in sixth grade when he found out I liked dogs, so he stole a copy of *Dog Fancy* from the library and gave it to me? What about the time I saw him slam his head repeatedly against a cafeteria table just to make someone laugh? What about the way I laughed? What about the things I didn't do because of the things I couldn't know? If only Sarah and I had looked in the right direction, maybe we could've seen him in his backyard all those years before he died. If only we'd known where to look, if only we'd been kinder.

Clark on the ocean floor: *Walking toward the dark mass, I got close enough to see that it was a cluster of rocks. It had holes in it like windows, and lovely lavender sea anemones, abalones, shell-fish, and sponges decorated it . . . I decided not to get too close. I walked around it.*

*You don't have to hide,* I often tell people right before I hide. Sanity is a way of seeing the world and comprehending it, understanding its scope. I see a glimpse, then turn away. But I imagine madness is a way of seeing everything at once. One does not *become* mad, one *goes* mad, like a place, like a museum where all the paintings are real and nothing is roped off.

Last year, I became convinced that I'd lost a tampon inside myself. I panicked in the morning when I reached down and couldn't find a string—I was sure I'd put one in the night before. I pushed my fingers up and became repulsed by my own texture, like taste buds on a tongue. How do other women learn to love their bodies? I feel that I missed out on some phase or lesson. I resent my opening and regard it as nothing more than a liability. And here it was again, causing trouble.

I couldn't feel anything, but I knew it was there. I asked Mark for help, which embarrassed both of us. I lay on my back and tried to breathe as he reached inside. He looked at the headboard behind my head, the way a woman looks ahead of herself as she feels around for keys inside a purse. I'd never felt so empty and large in my entire life—I thought maybe he'd just leave his arm inside me, that it'd be easier. Finally, he concluded that he couldn't feel anything either, but I swore I could still feel it.

A few hours later, a doctor at Planned Parenthood confirmed the same thing: there was nothing. I'd imagined the entire thing. I felt as if I might be going *mad*, in the old-fashioned sense of that word, the definition in which a woman gets sent away, locked up. What did the Greeks say about my uterus? I couldn't remember.

When I asked Mark what color of polish I should get at the nail salon, he asked, *Could you get, like, a chrome color? So that if you looked down at your hands, it would be like ten little mirrors?*

*One tug on the signal cord by the diver tells the tender, "I'm all right."*

At a New Year's Eve party in high school, my friend and I danced to the song about milkshakes. When the song ended, he pressed a button and made it play again, then he made it play a third time. Finally, the owner of the house said, *Stop, dude; I made a playlist.* My friend said, *No one wants to hear that; we just want to hear this one song.* That's one way to delay a year—we liked this one just fine, we liked our song. At midnight, though, we heard another one.

Sometimes, I record audio letters and e-mail them to my friend who lives on the other side of the world. A few months ago, I recorded myself during the eclipse. *I'm watching it on my roof right now,* I said. *The moon is obscuring itself,* but that wasn't right—it was just becoming a shadow version of itself. It was covering up its usual face. For a moment I saw

a prism effect, as if a piece of glass was shining through it—
so many colors at once. And then, like everything at the
end: red.

When I was about five years old, there was one chair my
mother never wanted me to touch. It had belonged to her
late father, but it was emerald-green velvet and all I wanted
to do was crawl all over it. At the same time, I couldn't stand
the sound of my mother's scolding voice, so I'd get on the
chair and call to her, *Don't tell me! Don't tell me.* And then
she'd come in from the other room and tell me.

I won't make any more promises. I also won't try to solve
you.

There.

I think that's my last promise.

# The Id Speaks, Mid-Transformation

This is my year, finally—the year of extremes. The leaders aren't just bad, they're tyrants; the polar ice caps aren't just melting, they're gone; the songwriters of the world aren't just fading, they're dead; the moon isn't just large, it's super; my bank account balance isn't just low, it's meaningless. I see only what's in front of my face.

In your bed this morning, I turned on my right side to look at you lying on your back. I cupped my left hand to make a semicircle against your profile and said, *I'm gonna put you on a coin one day.* Secrecy is our currency, and we're spending it quicker than we can make it. These days I feel sickened by fragility and tiptoeing—I want to be ruined by something for once. You pointed at the mole beneath my left breast and said, *This is my Polaris*, and I believed you. We crossed our fingers and our hearts and went north and hoped to die. I try to find solace in art instead of you—seems like a better idea—but I can't, not all the way. Art is ephemeral; I can't touch it the way I touch you, measure you, report you. We want to assume the forms of each other, to trade bodies—I leave my life and become you. I have so much hope I don't even know what I hope for. *I might be better as an idea*, you said, and it was hard not to agree—everyone is better in theory.

I once loved a stranger's specificity more than his lust: each action was written out for me and presented as fact, as if it had already happened—what could I do besides go through with it? I believed in momentum more than I believed in myself, and there I was, thrown.

My love feels so good when I aim it at an untouchable person, but then I always touch them. You said once that my love kept you alive—*No pressure.* I want to say, *You made me a liar,* but that's not true; you made me alive. I chose to lie in order to keep you out of the picture of my life as everyone else knew it. That's how I thought I could make you last longer, and I believe I was right. It's an honor to be so distracted, so consumed, to leave my mind, my priority— forget me, my love, and I will come back, back, back. I long to mark your bed, to make it mine. I want to be the one you remember.

I like going out alone, so that I'm accountable to no one—I leave without saying goodbye, I keep things for myself, I make memories my own. I find myself looking down on conventional love—my friends and their safe bets. They can't know what I know. If they did, I'd see it in their eyes. My fire wakes me up in the middle of the night. I don't know, I suppose I let it.

I told you I was moved to tears by a speech a former president gave. It's not that I love politics or even the president—I just love to be convinced, to be guided into feeling exactly what the speaker wants me to feel. I give myself up to oration, to God, which is you when I let it be, when you say *mine* in my ear. *You changed me,* I told you, because it was the highest praise I knew.

In my dreams, I'm bad, but that must mean I can wake up and be my real self, which is good. Right? Dream logic seems fine for the year of extremes in which we live. I become crazed for no reason, I go to sleep without guilt after doing another terrible thing. There is a mystery to our badness—it's not the things we do but the ease with which we do them. *More than anything, I think I'm just surprised with myself*, I wrote in my journal. *Because now I know what I'm capable of.*

It's a favor to allow people to think they understand me. How could they, when I'm still so far away from even myself? I hear my own voice on a recording and don't recognize it, I see an older woman in the mirror and wonder who she is. The mystery of myself grows larger the more I try to solve it. I once thought of myself as a tangle of cords on the floor, buzzing, knotted, half–plugged in, a pile of electric potential. I thought it was better that way. Our fantasies are contagious—we catch each other. I forget which ideas began as my own and which I've taken from you. Who adopted whom? We simply *became* the other; it was easy.

I never would have thought I'd find someone who could keep a secret better than I can. It's terrible the way I can't save anything—nothing stays in the place where I put it. My love gets up, walks away. My career takes off without me. I can't match my emotions with logic, and I guess that feels good in its own way. I study your face as it changes in the dark—I hope a secret might appear, and that you might be distracted enough to let me unravel it right there, right then.

It's this level of belief in the impossible that allows me to believe in you, in us, in our lasting. We must want each other to break in a way—why else would we take it this far? We must like the idea of burning down our homes and creating one out of the body we share.

I told you once that there was a button inside your mouth, and you closed your eyes every time I put my thumb inside to press it. I was the only witness to that machine, and you were mine, and, for a while, we worked.

# Small Crimes

Bianca had the kind of knowledge other girls could sense in her right away—it was as if she had already lived her adult life and had come back to her thirteen-year-old body to tell us about it. The real world was something the rest of us pieced together using clues from television, our imagination, and the things we learned from girls like Bianca.

The first time I saw her, we were on a boat; she is the only person in my life I can say that about. We were on our way to a beach camp on Catalina Island, off the coast of California. I saw her sitting alone, but she looked comfortable about it, not insecure or lonely. She wore a backward baseball cap and had blond hair and leaned against the railing of the boat, looking effortlessly cool. I was with my friend Emma, a quiet girl like me—we only felt safe in numbers. Emma was friends with other quiet girls like her, but I was always drawn to people who were the opposite of me. If I couldn't be brave, I could at least be near their courage. If I couldn't make trouble myself, maybe I could be guilty by association. I saw Bianca on the boat and I decided on her.

The sky was overcast and the air was hazy as the boat full of unsupervised children arrived on the island. We all stepped off with bags the size of our bodies, causing us to walk clumsily, side to side. Our names were called out with cabin numbers assigned to them. *Chelsea—seven. Emma—seven. Bianca—seven.* It was how I learned her name. Once we got to the cabin, I complimented Bianca on her backpack, and we walked to the cafeteria together without

Emma. At thirteen, everything happens either in slow motion or in an instant. The boat ride seemed like forever, all that time before making Bianca my friend, but it only took me the length of one heartbeat to turn my back on Emma.

The first thing Bianca knew was how lame the camp was. It hadn't occurred to me yet, but as soon as she said it, I saw what she meant. The first thing they had us do was learn a song; the boys were all the way on the other side of the campground; and our counselor's name was Dimples. *I mean, they're treating us like we're babies or something*, Bianca said as soon as Dimples was out of earshot, and I half expected her to start smoking a cigarette. Bianca certainly had a physical allure, but she wasn't beautiful the way an actress might be—her face seemed weathered in a sense, as if she'd just returned from a long voyage at sea, which I suppose she had. There was also an ease with which she spoke— she knew it all. The fact that she could properly identify lame things made me worry I might be next, but hiding my lameness gave me something to do. The truth was I loved being away from my parents and the mainland (a word I'd just learned), and my hair was already crunchy with salt. I usually had to fight to be that alive.

The second thing Bianca knew was the plot of the movie *Welcome to the Dollhouse*, which I'd never seen. *So then he says to her, three o'clock, I'm gonna rape you*, Bianca said, laughing. She said it was her favorite movie. She didn't even bother asking me if I'd seen it—she just told me the plot from beginning to end over a chicken nugget dinner in the cafeteria. It was the first time I'd ever considered the path my food had taken to reach me: thousands of chicken nuggets had traveled across the ocean for this one meal so mediocre no one dared comment on it. Dimples's ears perked up when she heard Bianca say *rape* at the table: *What did you say, young lady?* Bianca said, *Nothing, god*—long, like *gaw-duh*—and reached for my glass instead of hers by accident. I stared at the lipstick she'd imprinted onto my glass: she left proof of herself everywhere.

In the months leading up to camp, I'd had a recurring fantasy of having my first kiss there. I only knew what a summer fling was from watching *Grease* at Emma's birthday party, but I knew the rules: it was passion with an expiration date. It was human heat inspired by earth heat, a kind of doubling that can only exist outside of one's real life. And so it did: I thought about it every night, as a kind of preparation. I could see it so clearly—the cavernous cliff we would agree to meet at in the middle of the night, the look of shadows across his face as he approached me, the way I would touch him and he would touch me.

But once I got there, I only cared about the boys as seen through Bianca's eyes. Who did she like? What did she want to do to them (always *to* them, never *with* them)? Who would she kiss if she had to choose just one? *Probably Thomas,* she said, and with that we left to find him. Our cabins were just yards away from the shore, but the boys' cabins were up and over the hill, a hike too dark to take at night but just concealed enough to do by day. When we got to Thomas's cabin, Will answered the door in a towel, said he didn't know where Thomas was, said he wasn't his babysitter. *Whatever,* Bianca said. It was as if she didn't even want the things she wanted. *What's under your towel anyway, Will?* Bianca asked, and added, *Chelsea's never seen a dick; let her see it.* I held my breath and felt the waves hold theirs, too—the unknown has that kind of power. It was my one chance to see a naked boy, but then Bianca just laughed and let it go, and I never saw a naked boy until years later, when it was a naked man.

The third thing Bianca knew was a rumor: someone had filmed a movie with buffalo on the other side of the island years ago and never bothered to take the buffalo back to the mainland, leaving them to their private multiplication. *So, what, they're just over there roaming freely?* I asked. *Yeah, there's like a hundred of them.* Bianca had learned specificity made her sources seem believable—she never said *I think* or *I don't know*, she was always declarative and certain. I didn't believe the rumor but I didn't say so, just asked her how we could get to the other side. *Here's us*, she said, *and here's them*. It didn't look far, but we agreed to wait until the last night, in case we got caught.

The fourth thing Bianca knew was how to put a tampon inside herself. As soon as I saw the plastic packaging in her duffel bag, I thought, *Of course*. It suddenly made sense why she seemed so much older. A woman at thirteen, decided upon by a timeline that girls couldn't know about but knew all about us. Bianca didn't even mention her period—that's how used to it she was. I wanted to ask so many questions, but I knew to keep them to myself. Someday I would have the opportunity to be casual about that specific shade of red. I had seen it in wastebaskets belonging to my mother, remnants of a miniature crime scene.

Bianca and the other lucky girls took their plastic packaging from their bags to their hands to their pockets with a kind of grace usually reserved for long-legged animals in the wild, a deer bounding through the grass out of sight, away from men. But the bathrooms were all the way up the hill, so one night, Bianca whispered in my ear, *Chelsea, get up.* I immediately knew that nothing was wrong, just that Bianca needed me, and my adrenaline pumped accordingly. I slid out of my sleeping bag noiselessly and met Bianca on the side of the cabin, where she said, *I have to pee.* I laughed— *You want me to come with you?*—but she was already walking to the water, so I followed her.

We pulled our pajama pants and underwear down around our ankles and then to the front, trying to pee at an angle that would keep our clothes untainted. We giggled as quietly as we could, a kind of uneven burst of breath more than anything. I couldn't help but think about how we seemed like the only ones on the island at that moment, how the moon seemed sufficient to see her for who she truly was: a mystery shaped like a girl who seemed like a woman.

The next day, the counselors led a group of us by kayak to a nearby cove. Bianca and I had chosen matching neon scuba masks and laughed at how we looked in our gear. We hopped into the water, and she immediately swam away to explore some deeper area, joking about wanting to find a shark. I stayed where I was, floating facedown, submitting my back to the sun, a star that already made me pink and would now make me pinker. How was it possible that I didn't see anything whatsoever in the water? Not even one fish, just seaweed waving back to mock me? Emma swam nearby, looking like my past, but I didn't dare say hello.

Teenage cruelty is singular in its ability to forget, and by then I was beyond recollection.

At dinner that night, Bianca talked about our upcoming buffalo adventure. *Thomas wants to go, but I told him he'd fuck it up,* she said. *Yeah, he would definitely fuck it up,* I said, happy that she didn't think I was going to fuck it up. Her bravery was contagious—the more she breathed on me the sicker I got. It never occurred to me until much later that I may have been in love with Bianca, it only occurred to me that I had decided on her and made her my friend and that we would never be friends outside of this place.

I wish I could say Bianca and I traveled through the night and the tall grass, desire clearing our path, stronger than a machete. I wish I could say we held hands or kissed or touched in some way as soon as we were alone. I wish I could say we came to a clearing and saw hundreds of buffalo with their backs to the moon, as if we'd discovered a new land, a new time. I wish I could say we lay down in the middle of the abandoned movie set and stopped acting for once. But the truth is we made it only a few yards past the boys' cabins before a campfire and a ring of counselors stopped us in our tracks. *What are you doing out here, girls?* one of them asked, and not even Bianca had an answer.

# When I Turn

One of my favorite things to say is, *I'm almost done.* As a child, it was with my long division homework or my weekly chore of cleaning the bathroom counters with lemon-scented Soft Scrub and an old sponge. In college, I was in a constant state of being nearly done with studying and counting down my register at the store that sold overpriced cotton shirts. In a way, I feel I've always been training for this very moment: this time in which I never really complete anything.

I'm still trying to find that concrete indicator of progress. I suspect someone else might be the expert on my life, might be able to see what I can't. Hope can come from anywhere, but there's one pairing that never fails me: beauty and impossibility. Last week, I decided my friend, Erik, was both beautiful and impossible, and I felt it save my life in a way.

*Are actors good people?* I asked him as we ate cheese and olives on the patio of a house in the Hollywood Hills where he was dog-sitting. He asked, *I don't know, am I?* And I asked, *I don't know, am I?* and then we were spinning, faced with our morality or lack thereof, and it was Hollywood, so it wasn't the right place to decide, anyway.

I hadn't been back to visit Los Angeles since I'd moved three years prior, but I loved the ways in which the city was so *itself*—everyone seemed to have the same television bone structure (good-looking but forgettable), and even my cab driver practiced his screenplay pitch on me (which was actually quite good).

I'm beginning to understand my curiosity as a form of destruction. I approach with my questions and my desire to know someone, but I always take it too far, stay out too late, get a little too close. I said to Erik, *I wonder what's blocking you from writing the next song*, and he said, *I don't know, but I have a feeling you're about to find out.* We barely knew each other outside of our work, but it had brought us together, and then it felt as if we could ask any question, so we did. Even the dogs, begging for cheese: *Are you a good girl?* I asked the terrier, and she ran down the hill.

We realized we both had green eyes and one of us called it a *curse*, but I think we were just looking for things we had in common, little ways to stay bound, distractions from the people we already loved, new homes away from our homes. A kind of need had already formed. We aligned our hands to see how far up my fingers went on his and then the champagne was gone and the dogs had gone to sleep and the only thing left to do was kiss. I felt I could handle anything, I wanted to fight, but the only available war in Hollywood was tenderness. I fought the only way I knew: with more.

When I met Erik for the first time, seven years ago, we shook hands in the backyard of a house party in Austin where someone had made a bonfire out of gasoline and two old chairs. We were distracted by the flames, but someone said, *This is Chelsea*, and Erik shook my hand and then he put his hand back in his pocket and I didn't see him again for seven years. I just remember thinking how self-actualized and whole he'd looked when I saw him onstage later that night in Austin, and I remember thinking I could never know someone like that, much less be like that.

I know it's dramatic to say he *saved my life*, but I don't know anymore, I don't know what I need. We met again at a time in our lives when we were both almost done—me with my book, he with his record—and we needed something forbidden to bring us home, a siren to guide us in from the sea. One of us had a beautiful voice, the other had a bonfire memory, and we rearranged ourselves until we forgot who was who. The setting sun made the sky look so new that night that I began to momentarily love nature again.

Isn't it remarkable the way knowing one person can alter a life? If you're really lucky, you'll find someone who reminds you of yourself. Not the version everyone knows, but the part of yourself you thought you kept hidden: now you see it in him.

When I was ten, my parents decided we needed a larger home, but instead of us moving, my father said he'd build it. Men can decide things like that. He'd worked in construction and said it would take him a year. Soon, he was putting men in the back of his Toyota pickup and pouring concrete in the backyard. I watched from the living room as the gray sludge oozed from the barrel and my father helped to smooth the surface. How did men know the things they knew? Once the concrete dried, my father went about building the rest of the room himself.

Last year, my father and I went to visit my grandmother in her nursing home. Her arthritic fingers curved toward her wrists, transforming her hands into something else—clawlike. I remember one Thanksgiving, years before the nursing home: I watched in wonder from the kitchen table as her gnarled hands opened cans of cranberry sauce. Becoming hungry, I asked, *What time is it?* and she licked her index finger before lifting it into in the air and looking beyond me, as if she was concentrating on a draft of air. *One forty-seven*, she said, and it took me hours to notice the clock behind my head. It's a gift to allow a child to believe in magic. I thought, *She must really know the world*.

In the nursing home, she repeats her favorite stories. My father knows most of them to be true, but then, every third story or so, she'll say something like, *I can't wait for eighth-grade graduation next week, I hope they pick me up on time*. Or she'll tell us about the baby she just had, and how cute he is, and how she thinks she'll name him David, which is the name of my father, who is sitting in front of her with his mustache and gray hair. She's in a kind of loop, but the light is beautiful and she is mostly happy and what else can I do but tell her I love her and then leave?

I've always equated completion with death, and now I become attached to ongoing problems as if they might carry me somewhere. I've always loved men I couldn't quite hold, could never fully understand. It was like loving the same stranger over and over again. I can't be sure I'm not still in some sort of loop.

*Careful with him,* someone who seemed to know Erik said, as if he were a dog that bit someone once. I remember the men I've loved who pawed at doors in the middle of the night. I'd stay home so I wouldn't miss it, I'd stay up so I could be the one. Men like that change their mind in an instant, and so they can only be held for a moment. I used to bake apple pies, as if it were the 1950s, and in a way, it did take me back in time. My days then were filled with slow-motion hope playing like a long movie as I braided the dough. At the end of the day, the pie was almost done and I was about to know if it was any good.

At a library talk about drawing, a woman raised her hand to ask a question: *How can we document the forms of people as they move in and out of view? How can we, in a way, keep them?* There was some good answer, but now all I remember is the question.

Parties have never saved me, but I've never stopped thinking they might. *What are you working on? Is your book done?* New York is great because everyone's too tired to hide their contempt, but they know they have to ask something. It's understood here that failure is contagious, so being *almost done* only works for so long. At a party at someone's rich friend's loft, the keyboard player said, *This is a song about the artist's struggle*, and then he played the worst song I've ever heard.

The summer I first moved to New York, it rained for twenty-two days in a row. In Arizona, where I grew up, it was all bone-shaking thunder and flash floods that sent even SUVs downstream, but New York had the kind of rain that endured. It was satisfying, really, to wake up each day and still feel the weather matching my sadness, as if the clouds had something to do with courtesy. I'd spent the last two years thinking I would fall out of love with my man in no time. My grandmother asked me if he was *the One*, and I laughed, knowing with all of myself that he was very much *not* the one. But I'd ignored the facts all my life, this was no exception. I was in love with a man who didn't love me back and it was often wonderful. But then he was really gone, and the rain seemed to mourn with me, and I started to think the pain would last forever. Even then, I accepted my life. *It will just be sad from now on*, I thought. This was the new way. I was so lonely I began regarding my broken heart as the most beautiful thing in my life. Soon after that, it was gone, too.

*This is how I want to remember you*, I heard him say, and then I was the one to keep the sound. Echo, echo, I use you as a thing to call out to in my sleep. I don't need an answer, just a name, just a turn of your head when I say it. I'm happy to be warned of beauty, but I will not listen. I aim my whole world in that direction, I don't care what comes after.

I pouted on the flight back to New York, thinking maybe I'd never see Erik again. Why would I? A beautiful thing is beautiful because it can disappear at any time, or turn on you, or you could turn on it, or you could touch a hand you don't know and feel religious. The poets of the world could be dancing in another room to pop songs and we could hear the overflow. The details are hazy, so I fill in the scene: one poet is on crutches; another poet is crying in the bathroom, saying the room out there is full of people she once loved; I'm about to take an airplane far away from him; X, X, did I say his name enough, This Is My Friend X. Every song is on the verge of ending but not every song is beautiful, every human is on the verge of dying but I am not in love with everyone. I am in love with temporality, with the way we looked at each other for one night.

Someone at the party asked me if I'd seen the *flower moon* last week and I said yes, even though I hadn't. I had wanted to see it. A lie can be a sort of correction. In a year, maybe I'll think I really did see it.

I'm afraid to lose the thing I decided could save me. He's a muse because he's something I can't control, can't fully write down. I see what isn't there, I hear who isn't speaking, I do not touch him, I believe him into being. *Mine!* I say, holding a thing I found. My insistence makes it even less mine, and soon I find I did not want to own the feeling at all, I just wanted to know it, and I do. (I knew you.)

But it's possible I never existed—how much does he remember? Was I photographed? Written down? Yes, yes. I arrange myself into different shapes until I'm unrecognizable, I write letters 'til I'm sore. This is why I hate goodbyes: I draw a circle around the thing, but never fully bull's-eye. This is not my exit, it's a consideration of removal. It's another language, it's a light not meant for us, it's a place where everything's about to happen—the room we both left.

I still can't believe my father built an entire room by himself over the span of a year. It seems like the type of thing someone would start and never finish. My sister and I watched him step by step, wall by wall, and thought, *When will he bring more men to help?* But I don't remember anyone coming to help after the foundation was built. One day, my parents simply had a new room in the house they'd lived in for twenty years.

I refuse to think of perfection as a useless goal. I try to be as smart as I can, as talented, as efficient, and with as little error as possible. I see now how two things can occur simultaneously: as soon as I approach something, I set myself back, I fuck up on purpose. Sometimes I just want to know what will happen if I do.

The first time one man saw my face in the daylight: *Your eyes.* I asked, *Their greenness?* and angled my chin toward the sun. *No, something else.*

*him*

I romanticize Erik in order to believe that it was more than a transaction: I take something, he takes something, we stay human, stay ordinary. But something happened that night—what was it? I was ready to unlearn everything, thought I'd stay dumb all week, drinking pink champagne alone in my room with the Do Not Disturb sign on the door handle. But then I was outside, and outside I'm always trouble, or at least touching something that feels like trouble. I saw what he saw in me and I felt stronger for it. *Accomplice*: the right word for once. We were in it together.

Thinking of him, I held my mug in my left hand and the teapot in my right. As I poured the boiling water, I mistook my hand for the mug, and, for a moment, time stopped. I kept pouring until my brain caught up with my skin and I gasped so loud the world shifted and my hand was bright red and I'd done the kind of thing that lasts forever.

But here, tonight, it's super-moon time, and I'm on the edge of the balcony, demonstrating my compassion, staying in debt, writing to my muse again, making art with the idea of his hand. Someone's saying writing is fake work, I'm pointing at green lights when they turn, someone's insisting it's real work. I'm remembering buildings and headlines and all the ordinary moons renewing me. I'm like a dog—I love to hear my name in other people's mouths; I'm like a novelist—I put it there.

I wrote to Erik for days after I left—on paper, in my mind, in my dreams. It was a dialogue, a carnival with all its lights on, a road trip and I was flying—what else did we want? I was almost done writing a book about my life when a novelist asked me, *What about fiction?* What about it? Erik asked me the questions of my life, and I trusted his vision of me or I trusted I could live up to it. Now all my admissions can be held against me and probably will. I like that about the world.

I can't say what will stick, what will be written down. I watched the news at the laundromat and it was just footage of a rock where a coyote might have been the night before. Someone said they'd seen it, and that was enough. I face a screen, I imagine myself on trial. I sometimes refuse to think of my behavior as *weakness*, more of a mistake in timing. Most things are like that.

What is progress, anyway? I used to think it meant growing out of something, that only then could I ascend. But what of my gazing at the open door or Frida Kahlo's painting of herself as a wounded deer? Five arrows lodged in her side, her antlers tall, her face stoic—less *Look what you've done to me*, more *I put myself in the way of danger, now I have these souvenirs instead of my life.*

Every time I meet someone who I think understands me, I think it must be the last time. Oh, if a muse could be a thing I already knew. Oh, if I could come alive just once in the life I already live. I signed on to a thing, and yeah, it was like a contract, but what isn't these days? What's the difference between affection and attention to detail? (One form of danger: two people who don't turn from each other.)

I dreamt of him again—a feeling more than a plot, a reimagining of my throat more than a commitment, but I pulsed for him with true intention and my blue heart corrected every proof. I was glossy-eyed, splayed out surgeon style, loved-from-behind style, pressed against a couch I hadn't seen yet. Yes, I will fall in love with a person I created. Okay, let's say you are a gust of air—so what?

I stopped expecting nature to save me a long time ago. I remember being nine years old on the San Juan River: my father, on a hike, pointed to the ground and said, *Look.* I saw nothing. He picked up what looked like a bone and placed it in my hand. It was the remains of some kind of exoskeletal worm that looked as if it were made of stacked rings. He said, *This whole place used to be water,* and I could almost see it.

During the Depression, my grandmother and her sister used to store fruit in their living room in Missouri. They gathered all the watermelons, cantaloupes, and honeydew they could find. There was more than enough, but if they put it outside, an animal might get to it before they did. So they lined the room with heavy fruit and ate it as if they were in another time. The criteria were simple: *If they were good, we carried them home.*

# Notes

"Pity the Animal" was originally published as a chapbook by Future Tense Books. It was republished as an Amazon Kindle Single, and again as an e-book by Emily Books.

On page 73, the Marina Abramović performance proposal quotes are from *Marina Abramović: Artist Body, Performances 1969–1998*, published by Edizioni Charta in 1998.

On page 77, the Marina Abramović quote that begins, *It's because I want to be a whore*, is from *When Marina Abramović Dies* by James Westcott, published by the MIT Press in 2014.

On page 86, the italicized portion that begins, *It is always wise to tie a bright colored ribbon*, is from *The Book of Wild Pets* by Clifford B. Moore, published by G. P. Putnam's Sons in 1937.

On page 86, the italicized portion that begins, *Under no temptation*, is from *Trapping Wild Animals in Malay Jungles* by Charles Mayer, published by Garden City Pub. Co. in 1922.

"Second Row" was originally published in *The Scofield*.

Sections of "I'm Only a Thousand Miles Away" were originally published under different titles in *The Lifted Brow* and *Sundog Lit*.

Most names have been changed.

# Acknowledgments

Thank you Mark McCoy, Dee Hodson, David Hodson, Libby Burton, Lauren Cerand, Sarah Manguso, Kevin Sampsell, Monika Woods.

Thank you Marina Abramović, Jo Ann Beard, Sven Birkerts, Molly Lindley Pisani, Ron Carlson, Megan Carter, Kerry Cullen, Ruth Curry, Asher Dark, Libby Flores, Christopher Frizzelle, Laura Childs Gill, Emily Gould, Dinah Lenney, Maggie Nelson, Jeff Shotts, Lauren Smythe, Shelly Taylor, Peter Trachtenberg, Eric Tran, Steven Trull, and the PEN Center USA Emerging Voices Fellowship.

## About the Author

CHELSEA HODSON earned her MFA at Bennington College and was a PEN Center USA Emerging Voices fellow. Her work has been published in *The New York Times Magazine, Frieze, Black Warrior Review, The Lifted Brow,* and more. She teaches at the Mors Tua Vita Mea workshop in Sezze Romano, Italy, and lives in Brooklyn, New York.